The First
Thousand Hours

A Pilot's Log

The **First Thousand Hours**

A Pilot's Log

Jim Kasparek

Pleasant Word

Pleasant Word (a division of WinePress Publishing, PO Box 428, Enumclaw, WA 98022) functions only as book publisher. As such, the ultimate design, content, editorial accuracy, and views expressed or implied in this work are those of the author.

ISBN 1-4141-0434-0
Library of Congress Catalog Card Number: 2005902500

Dedication

To those who taught me to fly, from the most basic to more advanced realms of flight. It was often hard work but always enjoyable. You helped open the doors to a fantastic new world. Your efforts were not in vain.

Table of Contents

Introduction

Visibility ahead of the cockpit and the cloud ceiling above were both getting down to legal minimums. Now and then, in some places, they were perhaps even below what was legal for VFR flight, meaning the airplane must remain free of clouds so the pilot can see where he is going. A heavy rain rattled against the windshield of the single-seat, single-engine Piper Pawnee agriculture spray plane. Planes like this are also called crop dusters, depending on whether the chemical being applied to the crops is liquid or powder. They are built for fair-weather flying, not for rainstorms and thus are not necessarily very watertight. Water found numerous small openings to sneak in and drip on my pants, onto the map that was clipped to the small clipboard strapped to my thigh and onto the floor of the cockpit.

Deciding this was not a good place to be in this type of airplane, I turned back toward the Camden, Arkansas, airport only a short distance behind, landed, and tied down the Pawnee. Then I took my small brown, well-traveled suitcase from the chemical hopper between the engine and the cockpit and checked into a local motel.

Next morning the sky was still completely overcast and leaden clouds scurried along just two or three hundred feet above the ground; it was not even close to flyable VFR weather. Stepping outside the motel every ten or fifteen minutes to make an official check didn't seem to be doing much to improve the situation.

I was delivering this particular new Pawnee, a PA-25, from Piper's factory in Lock Haven, Pennsylvania, to Brown's Flying Service in San Antonio, Texas. The weather was spoiling the flight schedule as well as running up motel and meal bills. Since there seemed to be no chance of taking off for some time, I walked down the highway at the edge of town to a small convenience store and browsed through the bookrack for something interesting to read to pass the time.

The rack was filled with the usual variety of Westerns, detective stories, science fiction, and assorted other types. Being an airplane enthusiast, only one book caught my eye, *A Gift of Wings,* by Richard Bach who also wrote the bestseller *Jonathan Livingston Seagull.* Bach also loved to fly and wrote many books related to aviation.

Later, back at the motel, I paused after reading a portion of this new book and considered why people other than those who fly would bother to pick up such a book and read it; the market seemed rather limited. Would the average farmer, carpenter, sales clerk, housewife, businessman, doctor, or truck driver find it of interest? No doubt many such people have ridden in commercial airliners or in small planes but probably have never flown in a small plane capable of carrying only two, four or six people. Yet, I have found over the years that many people like those mentioned have, or have had at one time, at least some interest in flying or even in learning to fly themselves. Perhaps you are one of those who wondered what it would be like to be the pilot of an airplane but just never quite got around to taking the steps to make it happen. Other things came along and crowded out the time and the commitment needed—things like college, a job, family, house payments, and other normal activities of life.

A Gift of Wings is not like a mystery novel with a plot and characters. It is simply a book in which Bach speaks of the time he spent in the sky, experiencing and enjoying the people he met during his travels, the art of flying and the beauty of our country as he flew over it.

As one who has also spent some time sharing that same sky, experiencing and enjoying the same feelings and sense of adventure all fellow pilots share, I came to realize while reading that I, too, had a story to tell. Not a story of many thousands of hours aloft, of hair-raising adventures, of military combat flights, of airliners or corporate jets flown daily by pilots all over the world. No, my story is rather a collection of many experiences to which people everywhere can relate, non-pilots as well as those who quit logging flight time years ago. It is especially for those who are new pilots, the beginners, those just starting to grasp the wonder of flight and those who really enjoy flying smaller airplanes—the more personal ones. It is interesting that pilots of the largest airliners often fly small planes, usually their own personal planes, to relax when not on the job. In their smaller planes, they can go when and where they wish, not as a schedule dictates.

This story is also written as an encouragement to people everywhere not to give up on their dreams but to pursue them and bring them to fruition so that, years from now, they will not have to look back with disappointment at the things that could have been. It often deals with seizing the moment, taking some degree of risk to see what more life has to offer.

As I read Bach's book, flashes of recollection of my own flights, even back to the beginning pages of my first logbook, came to mind and brought back many wonderful memories. It seemed reasonable, then, to try to put down in writing the experiences hidden away in the pages of those logbooks which now number five. Some pilots probably have logbooks with pages yellowed by age, going back to their very early days of flight. One of my logs has yellow pages too—but only because it was printed on yellow paper.

So, this book is partly for my own pleasure. It brings together, in story form, some flights that are only a line or two in the logbooks with information on the date, type of airplane flown, from where to where, time the flight lasted, and sometimes a few comments that help bring the flight back to memory. It is something our teenage daughter, Joy, might one day enjoy reading to learn more about her dad's earlier years. Beyond that, perhaps there are those who have just recently begun to learn to fly or who are planning to do so soon who can find some joy, some wisdom, some humor, some useful information that will make their flying more meaningful and certainly safer. Finally, this is a way of drawing all who fly closer together in kinship, from the novice to the long-time professional. Even the pros had to start at the beginning, to make many mistakes, some comical, some serious, but they all learned the basics and faced many of the same decisions the beginners of today will face one day, if they haven't already. Such a bond unites all who call themselves "pilot."

This book was actually begun several years ago then laid aside and just recently retrieved to be revised and improved. My personal flight time begins back in the 1950s, a time many can still easily relate to but also long before many who will read this were even born. Now sit back, relax, read, and enjoy.

CHAPTER 1

"Look, a Plane!"

*D*o you ever stop what you are doing when you see or hear an aircraft overhead, look up and wonder who is in it, where it came from, or where it is going? Or look at it just to marvel at the wonder of flight itself and consider how a person learns to manipulate such a craft whether it is a small trainer, a commercial jetliner, or a sleek military fighter? Today, with so many jets crossing the skies each day, people often never hear the sound from far away as they used to with the piston-powered engines. Often a jet can be practically overhead and gone before it is even noticed and the very high ones are seldom seen or heard at all. So common are commercial, business, and private aircraft today in most places of the U.S. and many other places in the world that people seldom give them a second thought or even a glance as they pass overhead.

When I was growing up in the small farming community of Haxtun, on the plains of northeast Colorado, just at the close of World War II, an airplane was a rare and fascinating thing to see, at least to me. But just why or how or when I first became attracted to those marvelous machines, I cannot really recall. When one did fly over our town, I would stop my play or my meal, run outside, and watch it until it was just a tiny dot against a blue sky and, finally, it was gone. Often the vigil continued after the dot had vanished in the hope that it would return, but hardly any ever did.

Right after World War II several of the men in Haxtun learned to fly, including my father, who everyone knew simply as "Kas." His real first name was Othol but almost nobody knew that and he didn't publicize it. The primary trainer at the time was the famous Piper J-3 Cub, a two-seat, tandem (one seat behind the other), high-wing airplane with only a 65 hp engine. All Cubs came painted yellow with a black stripe along the side of the fuselage and the famous bear cub logo on the tail. In those days, probably more people learned in the J-3 than in any other airplane. It was a fabric-covered airplane, easy to fly, and the panel contained only the barest essentials of instruments. There were no radios and, because it had a tail wheel instead of the tricycle landing gear found on most planes today, it made good pilots out of those who had to learn to take off and land in it. So it was at about age seven, that I began to get a close look at real airplanes.

The Haxtun airport, if even worthy of the name at the time, was nothing more than an open pasture at the edge of town bordering, ironically, the local cemetery, which was probably the source of a lot of jokes. There were no fancy paved runways, no lights, no control tower, and not nearly as many regulations as there are today. Crosswind takeoffs and landings were not really much of a problem because they essentially did not exist. Because the airport was just open pasture, the airplane could be aligned to take off and land directly, or nearly directly, into the wind almost all the time. Maybe time has caused us to lose a good thing when the old pastures gave way to asphalt runways, which have caused a good many pilots to skin up their planes and their egos trying to cope with more crosswind than they could handle.

Later, the airport was moved to a location south of town to farmer Dan Young's pasture and there it boasted not only a windsock but a couple of small metal hangars as well. Nothing fancy—the floor of each hangar was just the dirt of the pasture—but they did secrete and protect these machines for which I was beginning to grow attached in a strange sort of way. On warm days I would sometimes ride my bike the several miles just to be around them and maybe have a chance to see one fly.

One of my earliest chances to go for a ride was from the local airport in a brand-new Piper Super Cruiser, probably about 1947. That three-seat, red-and-cream-colored plane seemed to me at the time to be about the ultimate in aviation transportation.

My father was never in the military; he sold Chrysler and Plymouth automobiles as well as farm implements and parts to keep them operating. Exactly why he determined to learn to fly, I don't know. His instructor was Rex Cox, a former military pilot. Dad did not pursue flying to a great degree but did earn his private pilot certificate and even managed to talk Mom into going up for a short flight or two with him.

One incident that occurred at farmer Young's field involved another local man who shall remain nameless even though he has been deceased many years. It seems that one day this gentleman, who was rather short, landed too hard in the tandem-seat plane he was flying alone and the jolt to the plane somehow caused the seat supports to collapse. Suddenly the surprised pilot found himself sitting only a couple of inches off the floor with his eyes just barely able to see out over the bottom edge of the window as the airplane continued it's

3

landing roll! Fortunately, all ended happily and neither plane nor pilot was much worse for the wear.

Flying didn't last long in Haxtun after two of the local flyers were killed returning from a trip in poor weather and later the activity declined to the point that, for many years, there was no airport at all for the community. Airplanes were apparently looked upon as being inherently dangerous machines. Today, Haxtun does have a small airport once again and it still has only a couple of small metal hangars but does have two hard-surfaced runways and lights. Want to fly in and meet some of the friendly local folks? Just fly low over the town (legally low) and gun the engine a few times as a signal you plan to land. You can nearly always count on someone driving the couple of miles east of town to pick you up and probably someone will volunteer to take you back to your plane when you're ready to go.

Today, when a group of youngsters are out at play and a plane passes overhead and one in the group listens, looks up and says, "Look, a plane!" then watches until it is just a tiny dot disappearing against the sky, he or she is the one who will perhaps one day be up there doing the flying, the one called "pilot."

In the March 2005 issue of *Plane & Pilot* magazine, Major Glen Richards relates a time as a second-grade student (1975) playing baseball, a ball was hit straight toward him. While the crowd yelled at him to get the ball, he was busy watching a new F-15 jet fighter overhead. He finally looked down just in time to see the ball roll between his legs toward the outfield fence. Now he is an F-16 instructor with the U.S. Air Force.

CHAPTER 2

Orange Crates and Imagination

*T*he Indianapolis 500 race has probably had many drivers whose early association with cars was the models they built as youngsters. No doubt men who have stood at the helm of an American Cup yacht or captained a ship as large as an aircraft carrier or as small as a rowboat on a lake did something similar. Their earliest vessels may have been just a scrap of wood with a twig or dowel for a mast and a leaf or scrap of cloth for a sail. Later, they probably built models, some simple and others very elaborate with many details and perhaps were even remote-controlled. There is the saying, "The only difference between men and boys is the size and price they pay for their toys."

How many of today's pilots can recall when, as very small children, their early airplanes were nothing more than a couple of crude pieces of wood nailed together somewhat like a cross, one for the fuselage and one for the wing? More exotic ones may have featured some sort of tail surfaces, maybe a second wing and a propeller or maybe something like a juice can for a jet engine. No matter that there were no movable control surfaces, no matter that the wing had no aerodynamics in its shape or that weight and balance might have been so far off as to be disastrous. Whatever those pilots' and carpenters' nightmares may have looked like, just the addition of a child's imagination magically transformed them into streamlined fighters, bombers, gliders, or whatever one's fancy desired.

If a "real" airplane was the goal, it required a discarded orange crate or sturdy cardboard box for a fuselage, something for a wing, and a piece of broomstick for a control stick (also called the joystick). With crayon, marker, or pencil, an instrument panel could be created with all the instruments and radio equipment necessary in a matter of a few minutes. With such a plane, a child had a real fuselage to sit in and, with the broom handle control stick, could climb, dive, and turn at will. Aerodynamics were no problem because again the mind streamlined the orange crate or cardboard box fuselage, put the proper curve on the wing, and made the control surfaces function as they should.

The engine? It ran the way the pilot chose. Out of the mouth of the pilot came the sounds necessary to create the scream of a fighter in a dive, the droning of a heavy bomber over enemy territory, or a jetliner full of passengers bound overseas. Sometimes the engine ran as smoothly as a fine watch; other times it would sputter, cough and possibly quit completely from fuel starvation or the many other things that could happen to a real one.

In the past, thousands of youngsters must have zoomed up, broken through imaginary clouds, crashed, or made daring heroic flights in such wonderful creations. Then, perhaps only moments later, that same box might become a military tank, a farm tractor, a race car, and when something else seemed more interesting elsewhere, the creation was abandoned and became, once more, an orange crate or a box.

Saturday afternoon in the mid and late 1940s often found the local movie theater filled with kids full of anticipation for the day's entertainment. Fourteen cents (to the best of my recollection) bought a ticket to adventure, usually in the form of a cartoon then one part of a long serial followed by a feature film. A brief recap of the serial brought us up-to-date from last week. The new episode would begin, then end fifteen or twenty minutes later with the hero or heroine in some precarious situation—to be continued next week! A favorite hero of the day was Jack Armstrong, the All-American Boy. The full-length movie was often a Western with Gene Autry, Randolph Scott or Roy Rogers.

Sometimes, especially after a film about World War II, paper model fighter airplanes were available in the lobby and could be picked up for free or a small price on the way out. Such planes were printed on heavy paper in full color and might be American, British, German, or Japanese. All you had to do was punch them out, insert tab A into slot B, tab C into slot D, etc., and do a little gluing, including gluing a penny in the nose for proper weight and balance. Correctly done, these paper models flew quite well when launched gently by hand. Mine are now long gone but it would be nice to find one somewhere to add to the den as a reminder of those days.

As time went by, our home was often the scene of model planes under construction, whether of solid wood, balsa stringers and formers covered with doped tissue paper, or of plastic. The construction site was usually the kitchen table, the dining room table, enclosed front porch, or bedroom. I think the bathroom was about the only room that was not at some time an airplane factory! Of course when Saturday and housecleaning rolled around, one spot that was always mine to dust was

7

the top of the piano because it looked like a carrier deck with ten or fifteen planes ready to be launched. My mother wasn't going to move each one, dust, then replace it.

Frank Borman, Apollo 8 command pilot for man's first flight to the moon, stated (also in *Plane & Pilot* magazine, March 2005), that flying has always been important to him and that he began his introduction to flying by building model airplanes.

One type of plane I never did have was the control-line model with a real gas engine. That was something I could not afford and I looked with some envy on any kid in town who had one.

So it progressed, from sticks to the orange crates to the models. If I wasn't building models, I was drawing them, pausing from work or play to watch real planes that occasionally flew over town, eyeing them until they disappeared in the distance, then standing just a little longer.

CHAPTER 3

First Entries

*T*he logbook date reads 9/12/54, and the aircraft registration number is N1770N. It was an 85 hp Cessna 120 and my first introduction to learning to fly. Dad had driven me the thirty-some miles to Sterling, Colorado, for that lesson because at the time I was only fifteen and not yet old enough to drive. He was probably willing to make that drive because he still remembered his flying and had some idea of how I felt about it.

My instructor was to be Aaron White and while he and Dad chatted, I looked over the plane we were to use. In magazines I had read about a preflight inspection but I was not introduced to one at the time. It seemed a bit odd to me, but not wanting to question the instructor, I said nothing. Probably he had already done one but just did not introduce it to me right away. Perhaps he didn't really think this fifteen-year-old boy was serious about learning to fly.

After thirty minutes of orientation flight including flying straight and level and doing gentle climbs and descents and turns we called it a day, landed, and secured the airplane. My first logbook, the one printed on yellow paper, was made out and signed. Before we left, Mr. White made a comment to my dad that I happened to overhear, "He sure knows what they're made of," he said. Though I was short for my age, I'm sure I must have felt several inches taller on the drive home.

Before turning sixteen in December I had had only four lessons, thirty minutes each. Having to go so far each way for each lesson and only when my dad wanted to take the time to drive and then wait while I flew meant lessons were rather few and far between. Dad worked six days a week and could take me only during his free time, thus taking time from things he probably would rather have been doing on Sunday afternoons.

So now I think about our teenage daughter, Joy. In the summers she has been taking horseback riding lessons. Because she is too young to drive, I take her; it only takes about ten or twelve minutes to drive to the stables from our house. Then I, or my wife and I, wait until the horses are brought out, brushed, saddled and watered and everyone else in the group is ready. We continue to wait through the hour-long lesson and the necessary time to unsaddle and do all the other work needed before the drive home, so it takes at least two hours of time for a one-hour lesson. But, because she is my daughter I don't mind. I enjoy watching her learn to handle the large animal and she loves it, so I receive satisfaction from her accomplishments. And she knows I watch, just as I'm sure I was aware of my dad watching me.

In those two hours with Mr. White, however, he taught me how to do a preflight inspection, how to taxi, take off, climb, do turns, climbing turns and descents, some stalls, and some landings. It was work all right but every minute was fun. Learning in the Cessna 120 and 140, which were "taildraggers," was

10

a good experience. Many of the pilots being trained today learn in planes with a nose wheel instead of a tail wheel and may later take jobs flying larger aircraft and never have had the thrill of flying a taildragger.

An ad run one time in the *Trade-A-Plane* newspaper was for a tail wheel airplane for sale. It said that only "real" pilots (meaning those who knew how to handle taildraggers) need inquire and it brought a smile to know that I was included in that special group. Years later, that and other taildragger experience was to help me obtain summer jobs delivering factory-new planes from Piper's Lock Haven, Pennsylvania, or Vero Beach, Florida, factory to various places across the United States.

Birthday sixteen came along and Dad gave me a choice few guys have. He said I could go on with the flying lessons or have a used car but not both. For reasons not entirely known, even today, my choice was to take the car. Maybe because it was something I could use every day, perhaps because it would seem a bit unfair for my dad to drive me about seventy miles round-trip and wait every time I had a flying lesson. Whatever the reason, the flying lessons were laid aside until college almost three years later. In the meantime, my appetite for flight had to be satisfied with talking airplanes at school, building more models, and reading books and *Flying* magazine, which I first subscribed to in February of 1953 when a sophomore in high school.

Probably every person who has learned to fly can remember those first lessons, even the very first one. Whether that first lesson was in a J-3 Cub or a modern two-or four-place trainer with all sorts of instruments and radios, there was, no doubt, a degree of eagerness, apprehension, anticipation, and awe. A close friend of mine who is now a retired airline captain once told me of one of his very early lessons in a Piper Cub. Not

11

only was the whole realm of flight a strange new world to him but at one point during a turn the bottom portion of the door of the Cub fell wide open!

Now if you're not familiar with how the door of a Cub works, a brief explanation will give you an idea of why this would unsettle the nerves of a new student to the point of canceling any future flying career right there on the spot! A Cub's door is in two parts—the trapezoid-shaped top half is hinged at the top and the trapezoid-shaped bottom half is hinged at the bottom and they come together at the bottom of the window in the upper half. The door is long enough that one person can easily enter the front seat and another can enter the rear seat at the same time.

To have the bottom of it flop open would make it seem as if the whole side of the fuselage had suddenly opened up leaving only a thin seat belt between the new student and the ground below! The airlines could have easily lost a good future pilot from fear that day.

By the time one has hung around airports a few weekends and listened to some of the tales of various pilots' experiences during their first few hours of instruction, enough stories of humor, work, worry, tears, frustration, and rewards could be heard to write a book dealing with first lessons alone. Sometimes when the airport lounge has several pilots swapping stories, ask somebody if he or she remembers the first lesson or two.

One young lady, early in her training, did her preflight check and then, with the instructor beside her, started the engine and taxied out to the end of the runway. After checking out the engine for proper operation, checking and setting the instruments as needed, she opened the window on her side and, in a loud voice, called out "Clear" (normally done before engine start to warn anyone nearby to stand clear of the propeller). She turned to her instructor and said calmly, "You thought I forgot, didn't you?"

Unfortunately, many of those lounge or hangar sessions are found less and less in today's modern, all-business way of instructing and carrying on aviation affairs. Former airline captain Barry Schiff recently wrote of an occasion during which he landed his small personal plane at a larger airport and in the lounge found only smartly dressed young executive pilots absentmindedly watching television, each in his own thoughts but no friendly communication going on between them. Captain Schiff, dressed in a T-shirt and jeans, undoubtedly had more hours in his logbook than all those young men combined. They could have enjoyed wonderful conversation with him and learned so much if the camaraderie often found at smaller airports had been present.

CHAPTER 4

Student Pilot

*B*ulder, Colorado, nestles up against the foothills of the Rocky Mountains about twenty miles northwest of Denver. It is the home of the University of Colorado where I spent the first two years of my college education. What interested me most, however, was not the sacred halls of learning on campus or the sports and other activities associated with such institutions but rather the small airport at the northeast corner of town. Today the Boulder facility is much finer than it was in the midfifties. Besides having normal flight training available, there are also aircraft sales and gliding and the old grass runways have given way to a fine hard-surfaced one. Especially in the summer, it is usually quite an active airport.

In 1956 the situation was considerably different. The flight office was an old building on the north side of the runway and the main hangar was probably an orphan of World War II vintage, or so it appeared. Two runways existed, both turf. Landing to the east, which was normally the case, one approached on final over a small lake and, if on an early morning flight, directly into the rising sun. On final approach from the other direction, a small bluff drops off at the end of the runway and sometimes the wind churning over it could make landing challenging.

A pilot landing to the southeast on the diagonal landing strip had to approach over a row of trees just behind the hangar—probably the standard fifty-foot obstacle so often mentioned in FAA publications—and they gave excellent practice in short-field landings. This diagonal runway also was good for practice landing on a field that was not very level. Pilots needed to learn to follow the contours of the gently rolling terrain, holding the airplane just off the ground as it slowed to a stalling speed for touchdown. The trick was not to run out of flying speed just as the ground sloped away leaving the plane hanging two or three feet in the air and resulting in a harder than desired landing as a reminder to compensate next time.

Saturday or Sunday afternoons would often find me sitting in the grass alongside the runway watching others doing touch-and-go landings and seeing what to do and what not to do when my turn came. If I had spent as many hours on the books for the university classes as were spent at the airport I might have graduated with honors!

Real training didn't begin until the spring of my freshman year, May 1957. The plane used then was N36324, a Taylorcraft BC-12D, probably a 1946 or '47 model with a 65 hp Continental engine. The T-Craft, as it was commonly called, seated two people side-by-side rather than in tandem and it had a control wheel like the Cessnas instead of a joystick found in the J-3. It was a taildragger, fabric covered, with so few instruments they could be counted on the fingers of one hand. No radios of any kind were installed. The fuel tank was just in front of the instrument panel. A wire was inserted through a cork bobbing in the tank and the top of it could be seen through the windshield. The amount of wire to be seen indicated the amount of fuel remaining—very high-tech stuff! Still, it was an easy airplane to fly, very forgiving of mistakes, of which I'm sure there were many, and it was quite easy to land.

Most pilots are probably somehow still attracted to the plane, or at least the type of plane, in which they first learned to fly. It was easy to admire all the other craft on the field—the new Cessna 172s and the impressive new twin-engine Apache—but those were just in the realm of wishful thinking. That little one over there, the green and yellow BC-12D, that was mine, at least the one I was learning in, and that made it just a little more special.

Bob Jones, an ex-military pilot from the Korean War era was my instructor and his wife, Shirley, ran the office. Bob was to remain my instructor all the way through to my private certificate. As in all lines of work, there are those who do their job well and some who do not. I felt fortunate to have Bob as an instructor and even today believe he did a fine job teaching the basics. He went on to fly with a major airline later.

Anyone who is considering learning to fly should spend some time shopping around for the best instructor possible. Don't be hesitant about asking people at the airports who the outstanding instructors are. Getting the best you can will certainly pay dividends in the long run. You usually pay the same price per hour for a poor instructor as you do for a good one, so why not try to find the best? Good instruction is a key factor in becoming a good, safe, proficient pilot. The same philosophy will hold true of a person looking for someone to teach almost anything—music lessons, horseback riding, dancing, art, skiing, or shooting, to name just a few.

Age and the number of flight hours an instructor has may not be the only or the best criteria for selection. True, pilots with many hours may have had more experience with different kinds of planes, weather, terrain, etc., but that does not necessarily mean they are good at teaching others what they know. Some of the very newest instructors may have gotten all their time in a trainer and perhaps the only longer cross-country flights logged are those required to meet minimum requirements for a commercial certificate and the instructor rating. Yet these same people may have spent more time learning how to teach others in a manner that is going to be most effective.

Consider such things if you are ready to begin flying or if you are in need of an instructor for an advanced rating.

Finances may play a role in selections also. If a person cannot afford to travel to a distant part of the country and pay living expenses there during training, finding someone nearer to home may have to be a compromise. Some people are fortunate enough to have the funds to go to a well- known school in another state and obtain the best training available and the cost is not one of the major factors. As often happens in life, there are tradeoffs to make.

For the next eight hours and forty minutes of flight time, Bob patiently put up with my efforts to master, or at least reasonably well learn, the basics of flight. We went climbing, turning, slipping, slopping, gliding, floundering, stalling, and bouncing around the practice area. With time, all the maneuvers gradually became smoother, confidence was building, and the parts of the puzzle were coming together to form the whole picture of what flying was about.

Much of the basic training then was as it still is today but there are also a number of differences. Stalls today, for example, are taught so that immediately upon recognition of a stall, recovery to level flight is begun and that is all that is required, even on a flight test. My stall training involved holding the nose of the airplane above the horizon line, continually adding back pressure on the control wheel as the airspeed bled off and maintaining directional control by dancing on the rudder pedals so a wing would not drop and lead to a spin. Then, at the stall, when the airflow over the wing could no longer create enough lift to keep the plane flying, back pressure was maintained until the nose dropped and passed through the horizon line as the plane began its descent and tried to recover flying speed. At that point, back pressure was released and full engine power added for recovery. You had to be on your toes, literally, to maintain control. Good training!

There is good reason for not teaching the full stall now. Theoretically at least, if a pilot can recognize the impending stall characteristics, feel the vibration or sense the different feel of the controls, and begin recovery immediately, the possibility of a spin, which could be fatal at a lower altitude, has been eliminated. Because of the training I received, even many years later it was fun to go up and do full stalls and always feel in control.

Spins are no longer required to obtain a private certificate but they were in 1957 so the day came to learn the dos and don'ts of that particular maneuver. S-Day arrived after only four hours with Bob and it wasn't one I was looking forward to with great joy. The parachute Bob had ready beside the T-craft was required for intentional spins but I'm not sure it had a comforting effect, in fact it probably had the opposite. We did the preflight inspection, buckled up, and took off.

At a safe altitude Bob demonstrated a spin to the left—slow the airplane, keep the nose up slightly and straight with rudder. Keep coming back with the control wheel until it hits the stop, then, when the airspeed touched fifty-five, kick in full rudder in the direction you want to go. Wow! That first quarter turn went by so fast my eyes were still looking east while the rest of me was going north! Before recovery, with the nose pointed down at a very steep angle, I had a feeling of being in a rocket headed for a certain and very unpleasant rendezvous with the earth.

In reality it wasn't as bad as it seemed and recovery to level flight was made with all sorts of room to spare. Back at a safe altitude it was my turn to try a two-turn spin to the left and later some to the right. The more we did, the more enjoyable it became and the lesson ended all too soon.

Very possibly, being the one in control as opposed to just being a passenger along for the ride had a lot to do with liking or disliking the spins at first. Not knowing exactly what would happen gave a feeling of apprehension but later, being the one in control gave a feeling of much more pleasure and confidence.

Being the one in control of nearly any situation will normally give a person the advantage, give more courage, confidence, and satisfaction that things are going the way you choose. Leaders display this in their actions before a group of followers. Followers are not the ones in control—they do what the leader tells them to do. Followers often lack the confidence the leader has. Think about this in business, in the military, in school, even at home between children and parents. Not everyone can be a leader in all things but overall, leaders probably tend to enjoy life more; they have a greater sense of control and accomplishment.

Many years later, while giving flight instruction to a friend in a Cessna 152, we were doing stalls when he accidentally over-controlled and put the airplane into the beginning of a spin. Almost without thinking, I was able to take the controls and recover the airplane for him, a tribute to the good training Bob had patiently given.

With about eleven hours of flight under my belt (seat belt in this case), including the two logged with Mr. White, the first real flight plateau was reached on June 5, 1957. After a short session of dual instruction early in the morning, Bob stepped out of the T-Craft and told me to take it around and do three landings. Many people used to say one should solo after about eight hours of dual instruction but since nearly three years had passed since the first four thirty-minute lessons and not having gone through an "approved" ground school as many do, I felt things were coming along well.

The two touch-and-go takeoffs and landings (or should it be go-and-touch since one must go up before touching down?) went as beautifully as the day itself with the sun just starting its cross-country trip as it traversed the blue Colorado sky. After the third and last landing to a full stop, it was done; I had soloed! It was indeed a great day and just a day before it would be time to leave Boulder for the summer vacation!

Of course, most pilots who recall that first solo will probably agree that after having the instructor sitting in the seat beside or behind them for several hours talking, showing, correcting, cringing and crying, it's almost like he or she is still there when solo time arrives. Bob's voice seemed to be there all the way around the traffic pattern and even today, as I set up the plane on the downwind leg in preparation to land, it can still be heard repeating, although perhaps more faintly, "Runway, attitude, airspeed!" It's still good advice in any type airplane one is flying.

I don't remember much about university classes but it was an exciting way to finish the freshman year!

CHAPTER 5

A Private Affair

*I*n September, classes resumed at the university but the more interesting lessons continued at the airport. Certainly, much work with an instructor remained before obtaining the coveted private pilot certificate.

The first solo flight is a major steppingstone but means little in the overall scheme of becoming a good pilot. Just because a person knows his ABC's doesn't mean he or she can read or write. So it is with flying: the lessons leading to one's first solo are like learning the alphabet.

To be able to safely carry other people, to use all the instruments and radios, learn about weather, learn to read maps, and all else involved in safely flying a cross-country trip or taking a local sightseeing flight is like learning the more advanced reading and writing skills. How skilled a reader or writer one becomes depends on the amount of time and effort put forth to achieve a high level of proficiency. How skilled a pilot one becomes depends on much the same concept. In flying, however, the consequences of serious error may be much more tragic; a serious error in writing is seldom fatal.

Good basics are an important beginning. My lifetime professional career was as a teacher, primarily of French, and the same concept taught to students of French holds true—learn the basics well and the rest will be much easier. It doesn't take deep thinking to see that the same principle applies to almost any skill one cares to pursue. It is similar to constructing a tall building; with a solid foundation, the structure can be built to great heights but with a weak, unstable foundation, the building will collapse into a useless heap of rubble.

For the next few months then, the logbook shows much time being spent on practicing basic maneuvers and gradual introduction to new ones as well. Also during this time, the operation at Boulder had changed to include a new trainer so most flying was done in the Aeronca Champion Tri-Traveler, often referred to as the Tri-Champ. This was a two-place tandem, high-wing plane, fabric covered and fun to fly. It boasted a tricycle landing gear, more instruments than the T-Craft, including a real fuel gauge, and a radio for communication and navigation. The Tri-Champ was the first tricycle-gear plane I had flown. It also used a joystick. The throttle was located just below the left window on the side, as on the J-3, instead of a push-pull knob located at the bottom center of the instrument panel that the T-Craft had or like many of today's trainers do. Those things were easy to adjust to and the lessons progressed well.

Short cross-country jaunts became part of the curriculum as well as learning to fly into an airport that had a control tower and required using the radio for communication. For practice into a larger airport, we flew to Stapleton Airport, the predecessor of Denver International Airport. It was located in Denver bordering I-70 on the south and east of Quebec Street.

At that time it was still far from being the very busy airport that DIA is now but it provided enough action for one used to flying out of "cow pastures."

At first, some of the directions coming over the radio from the tower sounded like a tape being played at the wrong speed: "Tri-Champ seven zero Bravo enter and report right downwind runway two six right wind two seven at four altimeter three zero point two over!" It soon began to sort itself out and, like the spins, wasn't nearly as bad as it first seemed. Nevertheless, there are still tower controllers who give directions over the radio like they are in a contest to see how many words they can cram into a five or ten-second time limit. A pilot should never be too proud to ask for a repetition or to ask for a slower transmission.

A southern-based airline captain flying into the New York area (so the story goes) got directions over the radio to this effect: ". . . airlines three four cleared to Colt's Neck maintain seven thousand expect further clearance at one five contact Kennedy Appraoch now one one two zero point four altimeter two niner niner eight over." The captain calmly requested that the controller, "Say again," and the same directions were rattled out again at machine-gun speed. After a slight pause the captain pressed the microphone button and explained in his southern drawl, "Y'all hear how slow I'm a talkin'? Well, that's just about how fast I write!" Even the pros ask for repeats if necessary.

It has been customary for student pilots on cross-country flights to have their logbook signed by someone at each airport where they land. The signature serves as proof he or she actually made the trip and did not just take off, fly around, and stall (pun intended) for the appropriate amount of time then return to land, appearing to be one of the world's best navigators.

One such signature in an early logbook of mine bears the name of Larry Farnham and the airport was in Fort Collins, Colorado, where I was later to live for quite a few years. He had built a very special type of airplane and probably no more than a handful of people ever saw it at all. It was called a Skycycle.

One Sunday when I was still quite young—probably during a trip from Haxtun to Fort Collins to visit my brother, who was attending Colorado State University there—my dad drove us to the airport to see this strange machine as the result of a newspaper article we had read. Not only did Mr. Farnham show us his invention, he rolled it out of the hangar, climbed aboard, and flew it for us for a few minutes. Most pilots are pretty nice people!

The fuselage of the Skycycle sat on a tricycle landing gear but was so narrow the pilot did not sit inside but straddled it as on a motorcycle with his feet placed on the wing where it joined the fuselage. There was a small windshield but other than that the pilot was sitting right out in the wild blue yonder. The flight controls were motorcycle handlebars with the throttle operated by twisting the right handgrip. Ailerons were activated by tilting the handlebars up and down and the elevators operated by moving the column to which the handlebars were attached forward and aft. Rudder pedals were located atop the wing at the pilot's feet. It was quite an ingenious design. According to an interview done with the builder, the only time he felt uneasy about just sitting out in the breeze astride his aerial motorcycle was once when, after takeoff, he realized he had forgotten to fasten the seat belt!

Flying out of Boulder, cross-country trips for training included going to such places as Fort Collins, Greeley, Denver, and Sterling (all in Colorado), or sometimes to Cheyenne, Wyoming, and for a long trip, to North Platte, Nebraska. Out in this part of the U.S. pilots have a several advantages that pilots in many places lack.

One is the fantastic visibility; it is not unusual to have forward visibility of forty, sixty, eighty miles or more though, in recent years, air pollution problems have reduced the amount of times the eighty mile and more really happens.

A second is that on the eastern side of the mountains, out on the plains, in the farmland, section lines make it fairly simple to follow a course without great concentration. They are roads laid out in quite true north-south and east-west patterns, one mile apart (thus enclosing one square mile or one section of land) and only an occasional check on position is really required when the weather is good, which is much of the time.

Finally, there are the Rocky Mountains themselves. As long as nobody moves them, it is almost impossible to become lost or disoriented when flying over the plains east of them because they can be seen from a hundred miles away and since they run basically north-south, one can quite easily remain well oriented.

Flying in the eastern U.S. is a whole different ball game. This is due to the much greater limitations of visibility, roads that wander all directions, few outstanding mountain peaks to note, and tiny towns so close together it is often difficult to know exactly where one is, unless of course, the pilot is using the latest in navigation equipment, which can pinpoint the location of the airplane almost to within inches of its actual position.

It is still a good idea to have the proper maps and know how to use them to keep oneself oriented at all times during a flight. But even with proper maps and the knowledge to use them, pilots do get lost from time to time, or should we say "temporarily misplaced." Years ago, I became "misplaced" for about an hour.

It was during a flight to deliver a new Piper Super Cub from the factory in Pennsylvania to the new owner in Mississippi. Because I had started two other delivery trips within the previous thirty days by following the valley from Lock Haven to near State College then turning west to follow Interstate 80, I was confident I knew where I was going on the initial leg of the trip.

Climbing above some lower clouds at Lock Haven to gain better visibility and for a smoother ride, I took up the usual compass course that should take me toward State College and beyond. Later, continuing on that same course, I noticed that checkpoints were not showing up as they should. Nothing on the ground matched the map. Surely, somebody had moved the towns I intended to use as checkpoints—it couldn't be my navigation! I continued to hold the plotted compass course but nothing looked as it should. Because the Super Cub had no radios for either communication or navigation, no directional gyro or other navigation aides, everything was being done by pilotage.

Finally, some railroad tracks appeared below, though none were on the map where I was supposed to be flying. Now it was time for some serious IFR flight—I Follow Railroads! Knowing they must lead to a town, I turned to follow them and, before long, a small airport appeared just ahead so I landed to learn exactly where I was. It was early on a Sunday morning and nobody was at the office building but a diagram on the office door identified it as the airport in Hancock, Maryland. Maryland? I was not only off course, I was in the wrong state!

Suddenly it dawned on me what the problem might be. I ran to the plane, swung the tail around parallel with the runway, then compared the number on the end of the runway (a compass heading) with the number indicated on the magnetic compass in the airplane; there was a thirty-degree difference! I had simply failed to double-check the compass before departure, apparently figuring it had to be correct on a new plane. Wrong! Especially on new planes I was normally in the habit of double-checking things but this one had slipped by. Figuring a new heading to Wheeling, West Virginia, the first major city in the direction I needed to go, and adding thirty degrees to it, I departed and easily navigated to the new destination where the problem was corrected. Live and learn they say.

Back to the quest for the private pilot certificate. After about another eighteen hours of cross-country and more hours of practicing the basics, Bob signed my logbook indicating I was ready for the private pilot exam. For every certificate or rating I have ever taken, if memory serves correctly, I have passed the written exam (now called the knowledge exam), on the first try although I do not reveal publicly what all the scores have been. Let's just say the written was passed after the usual blood, sweat and tears most pilots go through and on April 18, 1958, I flew to Denver for the oral and flight tests.

The flight test itself lasted for an hour and thirty-five minutes and I felt that we had done everything in the book by the time we were through. All in all, it seemed to go well but it's hard to tell because examiners never let on whether you're doing a good job or not, unless, I suppose, one does an extremely poor job. They apparently take special training in facial and body expressions, or the lack of them. The gentleman who gave the flight test was J.H. Prendergast and his signature is followed by the letters CAA (Civil Aeronautics Administration), which was the forerunner of the present FAA (Federal Aviation Administration).

A new plateau had been reached. I was no longer a lowly student pilot but a full-fledged private pilot entitled to all the privileges of that certificate. A common expression is that getting the private certificate is just getting a license to learn to fly, which is quite true in many respects. The flight back to Boulder was in the Tri-Champ but it really felt more like being on cloud nine.

CHAPTER 6

Building Time, the Hard Way

From the private certificate to a commercial certificate is a rather large step in flying. The basic difference between the two is that with a private certificate a pilot may not make any profit on any flying done. Any flight expenses must be shared equally by the pilot and passengers. With a commercial certificate, a pilot may fly for compensation, running one's own operation or working for pay for someone else. Regulations have changed but in 1958 a minimum of two hundred hours of flight time were required to obtain a commercial certificate and that had to include a certain amount of cross-country flight time.

When my private certificate was issued, there were forty-six hours in the logbook; another 154 seemed a long way off, especially when so many times a single flight would last only twenty or thirty minutes.

At the time, I was still in college, at least my body was. Most of the time my mind was off somewhere on a cross-country trip. Even now I'm not sure how enough money was saved to build up time renting planes by the hour except that some luxuries, like movies or eating, had to be laid aside or at least reduced.

One of the things I wanted to do besides build hours in the logbook was to try new kinds of planes to see if I could fly them and do it reasonably well. There was no real effort to critically compare flight characteristics of one airplane against another—it was more just a matter of seeing each different kind as a new challenge to meet. In fact, after returning to Boulder after the private flight test, the next time up was in a plane I had not yet flown, a Piper Tri-Pacer. N8849D was brand new and seemed like a big plane after the two-place trainers. Not only was the engine more than twice as powerful as the T-Craft's but it would carry four people and had a few other goodies I had not seen before. The checkout did not take long and I found it a pleasure to fly. Some pilots do not have a lot to say that is good about Tri-Pacers with their stubby little wing but I had no complaints; in fact, the first airplane I would own some years later would be a Tri-Pacer.

Shortly thereafter, other airplanes start showing up in the logbook as the time slowly continued to build, an hour here, twenty minutes there. The magic goal of two hundred hours was still out there on the horizon somewhere. Aaron White, who gave me those first two hours of instruction several years earlier, checked me out in the Cessna 172 Skyhawk (N3934F) and a month later another quick refresher in N3754V, a Cessna 120, since it had been some time since I had flown a taildragger. I loved every minute of it and was so pleased to see the hourly figures in the logbook growing but at the same time was always a bit saddened as the total numbers in the bank account seemed to grow correspondingly smaller.

The famous J-3 Cub has been mentioned several times. I had never flown one until an opportunity came one day to do so in Greeley, Colorado. Many J-3s have been restored and rebuilt and still fly but few are available to rent. Fun to fly? Certainly. Fast? Forget it. The cars on the highway could outrun the J-3, especially if there was any kind of headwind.

The J-3 must be flown solo from the rear seat due to the weight and balance properties of the airplane. When on the ground, forward visibility from the rear seat is quite limited and the airplane must be taxied in a series of slight S-turns as the pilot watches out the side windows. On takeoff and landing one must rely more on looking out at an angle rather than straight ahead whenever the nose is up in a landing attitude.

If that antique is still flying, its number is N42657. This and other aircraft numbers are given in this book with the hope that some of them at least are still flying and it would be good to hear from the owners to catch up on a bit of their history.

Another airplane that is now rarely seen is the L-2 Taylorcraft which is quite similar in many respects to the J-3. The particular one that came into my experience was NC52178. It was jointly-owned by several students attending Spartan School of Aeronautics in Tulsa in the late fifties. One of those joint-owners was the same friend mentioned earlier who had the door of the J-3 Cub open in flight and who went on to become a captain for Frontier and Continental Airlines. His name is Clyde Ruch, probably known to many senior pilots who were based in the Denver and New York areas. We still keep in touch. In high school we used to spend too much time talking airplanes and too little time doing homework.

Clyde and his partners were using the L-2 as a time builder while going through aviation schooling and had it based at the Harvey Young Airport. During a break from college (I had transferred to the University of Northern Colorado in Greeley), I drove to Tulsa to visit Clyde and his wife, Beverly. We flew the L-2 a bit just for fun. It, too, had just a 65 hp engine and was not a great performer but a kick to fly.

That was his first airplane. Later, after graduating with excellent grades, Clyde went on to become a corporate pilot flying an early model Beechcraft Bonanza and also the twin-engine Beech 18. After that, working for the airlines as his career, he had the wonderful opportunity to fly some of the now famous earlier airliners such as the Douglas DC-3 and the Convair series. From there, he moved up to the jet age flying the solid Boeing 727 and the MD-80. His son, David. also became an airline pilot and was flying as first officer on the Boeing 747 when a medical problem ended his professional flying. Clyde and Beverly are now enjoying their retirement home in the mountains near Estes Park, Colorado.

Checking the logbooks, a Cessna 140 shows up next. The main difference between the 120 and the 140 is that the 140 had flaps and an electrical system, that the earlier 120 did not have. Many of those early-model Cessnas are still very actively flying today.

Also in the Cessna lineup was the 175 Skylark, which was not manufactured very long but was, in my opinion, a good airplane. It was unique in that it had a geared propeller that could turn at a higher rpm than the engine was turning. This is one of several types I flew only a few hours but with each new or different plane there was a new challenge, new things to learn, new skills needed.

By now, 1960 had rolled around and, with a college diploma in hand, I began teaching at Lincoln Junior High School in Fort Collins. A lot of people seem to think that teaching students of that age group takes more nerve than learning to do spins in an airplane! At the time, I was flying out of the old airport in Fort Collins, on property owned by Colorado State University. The university maintained a flying club and did accept

34

as members a few people who were not CSU students or staff so I became a member.

At that time they had a four-place Cessna 170, which was a taildragger. Similar to the smaller 120 and 140, it carried four people. It was one of my favorite planes to fly but I was unable to fly it much for a couple of reasons. First, it cost more per hour to fly without others along to share expenses. Second, it seemed to spend a lot of time in the shop for one reason or another.

Every now and then, the club held contests to see if everyone was really as good a pilot as he or she led others to believe with stories on the ground. The contests helped keep everyone honest when it was time to demonstrate what one really could or could not do. Contests were always a lot of fun and a lot of people took part. A contest at a small airport is an activity one seldom hears about these days. They do sharpen one's flying skills and create lots of camaraderie among the pilots and spectators.

One reason the favorite 170 was sometimes in the shop relates to this incident I witnessed at a club contest during a spot landing activity. A CSU student touched down on the runway, rolled a short distance, then ever so gently, the tail came up and up and up. The nose went down and down and down and soon the prop stopped going around and around and around as it chewed into the ground. The tail kept coming over and in a few seconds our beautiful plane was lying flat on its back! The only damage to the pilot was to his pride and having a hundred or so people watching the whole thing no doubt made that injury much worse.

At home, I have two small plaques for placing first in two different contests. I've never won much of anything in my life and especially not in sport competition so these mean a great deal. One was awarded for a spot-landing contest and the other for bombing—flour bombing, that is.

For readers not familiar with a spot-landing contest, basically it worked like this: three lines were made across the width of the runway at the approach end, approximately ten yards apart, similar to lines on a football field. Contestants took off, flew around the field (or the "patch" as it is sometimes called), and tried to land so the main wheels first touched the middle line and the plane stayed on the runway without bouncing. Certain rules had to be followed during the approach to landing; for example, once power was reduced to start the glide, it could not be applied again or the contestant would lose points or be disqualified. Flaps could be put down but then could not be changed without penalty. Touching the wheels on the runway before the first line or not touching until after the third line was passed were also causes for disqualification. Judges measured from where the wheels first touched to the middle line. A pilot usually got three chances and the score was the average distance from the center line for three tries.

Flour bombing was another popular contest event. For this, a target was placed at some point on the field, preferably a good safe distance from spectators, parked airplanes, cars, hangars and stray dogs! The target might be a bull's-eye with one or two rings around it, each given a point value. Sometimes a barrel was placed in the center to see if anyone could drop the bomb into the barrel. Actually, standing in the barrel was probably the safest spot on the field from which to watch! Usually, each plane had a pilot and bombardier although some pilots preferred to do both jobs. Each plane carried three "bombs"—paper sacks filled with about a pound of white flour or lime.

Once in the air, the planes were required to remain at or above a specific altitude, usually two or three hundred feet, or be penalized. On each of three passes over the target, one bomb was dropped out the window and when it hit and burst, judges measured the distance from that spot to the target center. Hitting the target was not as easy as it might seem. The bombardier needed to allow for the altitude and speed of the aircraft, the distance the bomb would fall forward, and also allow for any side drift which might be caused by wind. If the speed was different on each run or if the altitude varied, or the wind changed slightly, the drop might not be anywhere close to where a previous drop landed. (The famous Norden bombsight of World War II was not allowed!)

Other little problems interfered too. In one contest, I was the pilot and was approaching the target (so I believed) which was a rusty-colored barrel. The plane was well lined up when suddenly the "barrel" moved and a quick maneuver was required to get back on track! The "barrel" I was aimed at was in reality the rear end of a rusty-brown-colored cow! On another occasion, I happened to be the bombardier and the plane was a Cessna 150. We were closing in on the target, my arm and sack out the window ready for release. At the proper instant I threw the sack down hard—but it never made it to the target at all. It simply smashed against the plane's entry step and fell to earth as dust—not easy to measure!

In January of 1961 the logbook showed a total of one hundred hours and eleven different airplanes flown. At this rate, I'd be an old man before logging the two hundred hours needed for the commercial certificate!

There are many different ways a pilot can log flying time— some easy and some not so easy. One solution would be to join the military and let Uncle Sam pay for the flying. That can have a lot of advantages such as fine training, chances to fly a variety of aircraft that most pilots only dream about, and getting paid to do it. There are some drawbacks, such as getting shot at or shot down if the flying is done in combat, having to do things the military way and much moving around the country or the world, which is hard for a family person.

One can also learn by going out and buying a plane and learning to fly that one. That's fine for the kid born with a silver spoon in his mouth but difficult for the average young person to do, especially in today's economy. Another possibility is to purchase a plane in partnership with one or more other pilots and I have done that twice. Some freedom is lost in a partnership since the plane cannot be available to all partners at all times. The beauty of a partnership lies in the lesser amount each needs to pay to own, to insure, and to maintain the airplane. Most people who are newer pilots will rent aircraft to fly and pay by the hour which is what I did for quite a long time but this method also rapidly punches holes in the bank account.

The next thirty-five or forty hours that appear in the logbook are not very exciting with perhaps two or three exceptions. Most flights were local and lasted about thirty minutes each. A few were cross-country but they were short. Back then, a flight of twenty-five miles or more in a straight line from the departure airport could be counted as cross-country. Today that is not true. The distance required is now greater because of faster aircraft and improved navigational equipment.

During this time the Piper Colt was also added to the list of planes flown. The Colt is similar to the Tri-Pacer but has only two seats, side-by-side, a smaller engine of 108 hp and no wing flaps; it also was fun to fly. In fact, to the best of my recollection, all planes were fun to fly, none so bad it was crossed off the list as unacceptable.

Even on the local flights, however, I did a lot of practicing on the basic maneuvers in order to be well prepared when the day for a commercial test arrived. In a sense, nearly all flying is really doing the basics—takeoffs, climbs, descents, turns, maintaining course, speed and altitude, and landings. It is true even with the airliners. Even an approach to a landing under instrument conditions (IMC) uses all the basics during the approach procedures and involves other elements, making it more complex than a landing in clear weather. In such a situation, it is very important to know how to fly the airplane without consciously giving attention to each detail so attention can be given to other vital matters such as changing radio frequencies, writing information received from the controllers and monitoring essentials like time, fuel, temperatures, and landing gear.

The next time you fly, you might test yourself briefly on a few basics. Can you maintain a selected altitude within the limits you set for yourself, whether one hundred feet, fifty feet, or ten feet? Can you maintain a compass heading within limits you set? Can you climb or descend at a predetermined rate of so many hundred feet per minute? These and other little tests you can do in a matter of a few minutes will do much to sharpen your skills. Anybody can be a sloppy pilot but it takes practice to be a good one.

One cross-country trip during this time involved a trip from Sterling, Colorado, to Minden, Nebraska, to see an air show, one of my first. A couple of friends went along and shared expenses, which helped a lot and having company made such trips more enjoyable. Sometimes it is nice to be alone in flight and at other times it is pleasant to be able to share one's experiences with others. The show was put on by the Cole brothers and it was a privilege to watch Duane Cole fly. He authored several books on flying and at the time was considered one of the best in the business. In early 2005 he passed away, having logged more than thirty thousand hours.

Prices have changed a lot since all this was being done but then so have incomes. In 1961 the average rental price for a Cessna 150 was about nine dollars per hour wet. Now for readers not familiar with some of aviation's terminology, "wet" simply means the fuel is included in the rental price; it does not mean the airplane was just rained on, just washed, or used by a dog in place of a fire hydrant.

So the time in the logbook slowly accumulated using the rent-by-the-hour system. Lots of notes in the log show practice on timed climbs, power-on and power-off stalls, forced landings (down to within a few feet of the ground before climbing back again), steep turns, eights-on-pylons, wheel landings (I always thought this was a clever name—how else are you supposed to land except on the wheels?), slow flight and so on. In all of 1961 the total time flown added up to a meager thirty-three hours, fifty-five minutes.

The summer of 1962 brought an opportunity to attend a foreign language institute in New Britain, Connecticut. I applied to several locations but one reason for applying to Connecticut was because I had never been to that part of the U.S. The only one to which I was accepted was in New Britain. In addition to the language classes, I was anxious to do some flying there to see how it compared to flying in Colorado. What a surprise! After a checkout in a new Piper Caribbean—an improved Tri-Pacer, a new world waited to be explored.

Several flights were made in N33082 along the Connecticut River Valley and a couple in another Tri-Pacer, N10335, out of Newport, Rhode Island—the hometown of my roommate during the institute. Newport was particularly fun to see from the air because of all the water and the variety of boats as well as the famous mansions, such as the Vanderbilt mansion, along the edge of the water.

My roommate was Bill Moody and his father was a well-known dentist in Newport. Dr. Moody had an unusual way of putting his children through college. He was a collector of antique automobiles dating to the very early 1900s. His cars were in showroom condition and from time to time he would put on his "duster"—the long white coat worn to keep one's clothes clean in that era, don his small-billed cap, his large gauntlet-like driving gloves, and his small round driving goggles. Mrs. Moody would sit proudly beside him, dressed in the fashion of those early days, including a large, wide-brimmed hat secured with a ribbon under the chin to keep it from blowing off in the open car. Together, they would take one of the antiques out for a short drive or sometimes to a rally where drivers of other antique autos could assemble and admire each other's prizes (their cars, that is, not their wives!).

When the time came to pay to put another child through college, one of the cars was sold to finance the endeavor. I always thought that was a pretty neat way to finance college instead of just putting money in a bank to earn some interest. It was sort of like having your cake and eating it too.

Several things were immediately obvious when comparing flying in Connecticut to flying in Colorado. First, because of the lower elevation of the land, which is basically sea level or very close to it, the airplanes required much less of a ground roll for takeoff and the climb was at a steeper angle. In Colorado Springs, where my home is, the elevation is about 6,200 feet above sea level and the air is much less dense, therefore requiring a much longer ground roll before takeoff and a much flatter climb angle. A second thing was the reduced visibility in the East due to several factors such as much more humidity, more industrial pollution, and more pollution from cars, trucks, and buses. I learned that instead of a normal horizontal visibility of fifty miles or more which is common in the West, ten miles is considered very good in the East in many areas.

Not only was there the feeling of not being able to see well where I was going in the air but there was the distinct feeling something was wrong on the ground as well! With so many trees, it was like flying over the Amazon jungle and there was not a straight road to be seen anywhere—nothing like following the section lines in Colorado, Nebraska, or Kansas that run straight for perhaps fifty miles or more with hardly a kink in them. To make matters worse, the trees hid all the smaller towns and trying to keep track of one's position was an exercise in frustration to a "foreigner." Out West, a pilot can be miles off course and still spot a town without difficulty and identify it without much of a problem.

Please don't misunderstand—the scenery was great and I loved every frustrating minute flying over that part of the country. It was just so different from what was normal for me. After some aerial exploring, sometimes it was a challenge just to find the way back to the airport where I started. Using VOR navigation did simplify things a lot, however. I have had the opportunity to fly in areas along the West Coast as well—to San Diego, L.A., and in the Seattle, Washington, and Portland, Oregon, areas, and found many of the same conditions as were seen in the East.

If you, as a pilot, have never flown in a part of the country that is considerably different than where you normally fly, I would strongly suggest you do so whenever possible. You will be delighted at the differences and the challenges, and become a better pilot for the experience. Don't put it off if you have a chance to go.

Two more planes show up in the logbook now; both were "just for fun," just to try something different. One was N3016G, a Fornaire Ercoupe, based on the earlier Aircoupe. Built by

Forney Industries in Fort Collins, Colorado, the Ercoupe was a tricycle-gear, low wing, two-seat airplane with twin vertical stabilizers and no rudder pedals because the rudder and ailerons were interconnected. It also featured a bubble-type canopy that could be left open in flight, making flying much like driving an aerial convertible car. The second was N5010W, my introduction to the Piper Cherokee line. It was a Cherokee 140 rented at Boulder and was the four-place version with a 160 hp Lycoming engine.

Two entries in September of 1964 are of particular interest because they took place in England. Two of my teaching years were with the Department of Defense school system. The first was spent in Newfoundland, which accounts for a long period of time with no flying. The second was at Wethersfield Air Force Base about forty miles north of London in Essex County, a farming area. The base at that time had a flying club that I was eligible to join as a result of being on the faculty of the base school. Needless to say, no arm-twisting was needed to get me to sign up.

Unfortunately, the club airplanes did not include the Air Force F-100 Super Sabre jet fighters that were based there and were the hottest thing going at the time, so we had to settle for a Piper Tri-Pacer and an older Cessna 140. To my dismay, I was able to fly each only one time during the nine months I lived there. The rest of the time they were not available when there was time in my schedule or they were in the shop for maintenance. Perhaps I should feel fortunate to have had the experience, however brief.

Flying in England was very much like flying in the Connecticut area—lots of haze, many tiny villages, mile after mile of trees and tiny farm fields and not a straight road in sight. I heard of an Air Force colonel flying one of the club planes who got very lost on a cross-country trip of only about forty miles! Once I had an opportunity to see the countryside from the air, it was certainly easy to see how that could happen if one was flying just by pilotage (using no radio equipment for navigation). Maybe the good colonel was used to flying in some of the Great Plains or Western states also. If the opportunity comes again to see some of Europe from the air in a small airplane, I think I would jump at the chance.

You have read that many roads in the plains states and the West run straight for many miles. Shortly after our arrival at Wethersfield, the whole staff of new teachers was gathered to hear a lecture on driving in England in order to prepare us to get our special driving licenses. The officer speaking warned us that if we ever found ourselves driving on a straight stretch for more than about a hundred yards to get the car off of it because we were probably on the base runway instead of the road. One day, just for fun, while driving to a town only about nine miles from Wethersfield, I counted approximately fifty curves of some degree in the road!

Because of the two years with the Department of Defense schools, the logbook shows only six hours, fifty-five minutes flown in 1963 and only two hours, fifty minutes in 1964. Something had to be done about that and that is where N602A enters the picture.

CHAPTER 7

*P*robably a lot of people wouldn't call her pretty but in my eyes she was one of the prettiest in the world because she was mine. If "she" was a pretty girl it would have been even better; my "she" was a late 1951 Piper Tri-Pacer, registration number N602A (November six zero two Alpha), sitting in the dirt at Tulsa's Harvey Young Airport and I had come to take her home.

My friend, Clyde, still in aviation school at Spartan, had gotten word of the airplane being for sale. He knew the missionary who owned it and who would soon be going back to South America and wished to sell it. Airplane drivers are a unique bunch of people in some ways and I was surely as unique as any. As soon as my summer college class was over in Greeley, I jumped into the little British Sunbeam Alpine sports car purchased during my year teaching in England and headed for Oklahoma to see what this man had to offer. After an all night drive, a couple of hours sleep in the car—like trying to sleep in a very small closet—and a quick bite to eat, I headed to Harvey Young for a first look.

The gentleman who owned the airplane told me a bit about it, showed me the location of all the switches and knobs and we cranked up the engine for a short hop. No doubt my mind was pretty well made up even before the flight. Still, I did want to see what the asking price would buy.

Normally, I would have taken considerably more time to inspect the aircraft, spend a lot of time looking over the engine logbook, and getting other information from sources besides the owner. Because the owner was a missionary, however, I felt he was trustworthy, so his word was good enough for me. Nothing out of the ordinary showed up in the books or during the flight and within thirty minutes we had closed the deal.

Soon, the Sunbeam (sometimes referred to by my friends as the Mixmaster because of the electric Sunbeam food mixer with that name) was headed back to Colorado. My bank account was now $4,000 poorer but I felt rich indeed (that price was the full price, not a down payment).

The next weekend, I boarded a commercial flight back to Tulsa to pick up the new treasure. As mentioned earlier, some people don't have a lot to say that's good about Tri-Pacers, but for the year I owned N602A we had some great times together and, even though there were a few problems, there were far more good times than bad. N602A was originally a 125 hp airplane but the engine had been boosted to 135 hp, which was better for the higher altitude airport from which it would be flown in Colorado.

From Tulsa, the route home was via Greensburg and Dodge City, Kansas, and back to Fort Collins. To me, it was just about as good as having a brand-new airplane. If anyone reading this happens to know what ever became of that particular airplane, I would be very interested to know. Hopefully she is still flying

46

somewhere. If not, I hope her demise was a peaceful one and not tragic, although that may be the case as it is with many others.

Several advantages of ownership over renting are readily apparent. There is no scheduling problem and that means greater convenience. Your airplane is ready and waiting to go whenever you are. If an airplane is owned in partnership, which was the case with two others I owned, the owners have far fewer scheduling problems than they would have renting from an FBO (fixed base operator). Flying the same plane regularly brings familiarity, making various instruments, switches, radios, etc. easier to locate quickly both day and night which should make one a safer pilot. Should an emergency arise, knowing exactly where to find a certain light switch, the fuel selector or other needed item easily could be very important and make a difference in the outcome of the situation.

In the 1960s, restrictions over larger cities were less rigid than now. One day, while sightseeing in N602A over downtown Dallas, I apparently became so engrossed with what there was to see below, I forgot to watch the fuel gauges, but when the normally smooth-running engine suddenly began to sputter, it got my attention back inside the airplane in a hurry! There was really no big problem, simply a matter of switching the fuel selector to the other tank, but it took only a few seconds because I was familiar with the airplane and soon the engine was again purring happily.

Being the only pilot or perhaps one of only two or three flying a given plane also means it is easier to monitor how it is treated. When using a plane flown by many different people, one is never sure how it has been handled. An extra hard landing that might put undue stress on the landing gear or other parts may go unreported by someone else; after all, nobody wants to admit doing something that might not only do some damage to the plane but might also reflect on that pilot's capabilities.

Another advantage is simply being able to be around the plane often, to "tinker" with it, to clean it, change the oil, inspect it closely, do little jobs to make it look nicer, and be more comfortable. Doing such things helps a pilot learn a lot about the machine that renters may never learn. Pilots are permitted to do a limited amount of work on aircraft without being licensed mechanics. They are also permitted to do major work if it is supervised by a licensed aviation mechanic. Knowing what makes one's plane tick or knowing its special strengths and weaknesses can add greatly to a feeling of confidence in it. It also allows a pilot to recognize more quickly some small sound or feel or smell that is a clue that something is not quite normal and this could easily help correct a minor problem before it becomes a major one. Pride of ownership usually means the airplane receives much better care than a rented one, just as the car one owns normally receives better care than cars one rents.

The picture is not all roses, however. Ownership brings out problems and frustrations which renting does not. There is the matter of deciding on insurance: How much? Which company offers the best deal? Can I meet the airplane and insurance payments? The plane will either be tied down outside or hangared. If outside, weather creates special problems on both the airplane and the owner's nerves. I have seen pilots at the airport in the middle of the night putting extra tie-down ropes on in winds approaching a hundred miles per hour to save their birds. Sandstorms pit windshields and chip paint, which must be replaced. In winter, the plane may be covered with ice or snow that must be removed before flight—often a long, cold process. Summer sun may easily raise temperatures inside a closed airplane to the point that radios and other equipment are affected and upholstery or plastic parts may fade and crack.

Keeping the plane in a hangar is much nicer but more expensive and often the hangar may have no electricity or water available. Still, one needs to compare the hazards and potentially high expenses of keeping a plane outside with the hangar cost. In some cases, the higher hangar cost may even save the owner money in the long run due to less wear and tear on the plane and its equipment. A hangared airplane generally keeps its value better and that means more income when it is finally traded or sold. Even in winter, if the hangar can be heated to only about forty degrees, the plane's engine will start easier and with less wear on things such as gyros or lubricated engine parts. By increasing the temperature another ten degrees or so, the hangar can be a comfortable place to work on the airplane in the winter—a great advantage over working outside in the cold. When working inside, things may be taken care of more quickly than they might be if left for a warmer day or perhaps forgotten if the craft is outside.

Today, particularly at airports of larger cities, hangar rental prices have become so high owners are faced with the choice of paying those prices, leaving the airplane outside, or selling it. The cost of hangaring becomes so high, some cannot afford to fly the airplane.

ADs (Airworthiness Directives) are issued periodically and need to be complied with for an airplane to continue to be considered airworthy. These may be minor but can also be major repair or replacement items that may be very costly. The renter need not be concerned with these other than to verify that they have been taken care of before renting the plane. The owner is responsible for having them done and the expense could come as a very unwelcome surprise.

To own or not to own? Many factors are involved including the bank account, the spouse's opinion, whether you wish to eat steak regularly and not own, or to own and eat lots of soup and oatmeal. Maybe you just decide to buy and work it out without any solid plan simply because it is something you always wanted to do. Personally, I never regretted owning. But I was single at the time I was sole or part owner of all three airplanes and that could make a lot of difference.

N602A and I started bouncing around the local area and occasionally on slightly longer jaunts. I was thoroughly enjoying doing my own thing in my own bird. One day, at an air show in Sidney, Nebraska, the right magneto dropped off more rpms than normal during the pretakeoff engine check and the warning should have been taken more seriously than it was. Two days later, returning to Fort Collins from Denver's Jeffco Airport, the engine suddenly lost approximately 50 percent power. That made me sit up on the edge of the seat and pay attention! The decision was not hard to make—I might not make it home, about another twenty-five minutes, so I turned west and headed for Boulder, only about five or six minutes away. I left the airplane after explaining the problem to the mechanic and found another way home.

One month and $300 later I got the airplane back with not only the engine better (it had blown a manifold gasket) but a few other odds and ends as well. Incidentally, $300 in those days was a whole lot more money than it is now!

In February of 1966 the logbook shows the two hundredth hour and 602A still going strong. About this time the old field in Fort Collins closed and the Tri-Pacer was moved to a different base at the new Fort Collins-Loveland airport nearby.

Looking back through the pages brings memories of many fun flights, most local, a few somewhat longer. One day was just a fun day of "airport hopping" from one airport to another in

the Denver area with my friend, Clyde, just as he was beginning his airline career.

Shortly thereafter, following a fresh annual inspection,
N602A and I were off on a week-long trip, something not so
easily arranged with a rental airplane. This time, the trip was
first to Dallas (the time the fuel tank ran dry) to visit a friend
with whom I had worked in Newfoundland. From there, on
to Hot Springs, Arkansas, to visit my brother, Bob, who was
working with the National Park Service, then finally to Salina,
Kansas, to see an uncle and aunt.

What a wonderful machine is the airplane! It has been
referred to as both a magic carpet as well as a time machine
and it indeed does come close to being just that. From the air
one sees vast panoramas of the country from a perspective
that many have never had the pleasure to experience. From
on high, the countryside is pretty and clean, and even over
towns the unsightly trash and litter cannot be seen, at least not
most of it. Places that are far enough apart to be wearisome by
car or might not be visited at all because of distances become
easily accessible by air.

One of a pilot's greatest pleasures is that of taking up people
who have never been in an airplane in their lives. Giving them
a nice gentle ride and seeing the expressions on their faces and
hearing their comments as they "ooh" and "aah" at the sights
they see below or as they recall them later on the ground is
very rewarding. I don't believe I have ever taken anyone for
a first ride who didn't really enjoy it and did not express a
desire to go again.

On one occasion, a fellow teacher's wife gave her husband
a birthday present of a one-hour flying lesson with me. Once
in the air, he was so fascinated with the view of the land below,
he was not so interested in flying the airplane, he just wanted
to look, and he loved it!

Eleven months after I first saw N602A, we parted ways. The dates, both of purchase and of sale are outlined in red in the logbook because they, and other events similarly marked, are like milestones in my personal little world of flight.

Actually, the parting came in a rather unusual way. My savings account had starved during those eleven months, down to skin and bones, because it had not been fed once in the entire time. I decided that, as much as I liked the airplane, my money would be better spent on a nicer place of my own to live.

For some time the idea of living in a newer mobile home than the one I was in had been on my mind. Next door to the mobile home park in which I was living at the time was a mobile home sales lot. One day I approached the lady there at the desk and, when asked if she could help me, I explained that I would be interested in doing some trading but wasn't sure they would want what I had to offer. After explaining that I owned an older mobile home and a fifteen- year-old airplane to trade for a brand new-mobile home, I expected to be politely told to go take my crazy business elsewhere. Instead, she simply said "Come with me; I think the manager will want to talk to you."

The manager, it turned out, used to fly and had just decided to renew his required medical license to become an active pilot again. Naturally, his kids thought an airplane would be a really cool trade-in. To make a long story short, within a few days we worked out a deal for a straight-across trade, my older mobile home and the cherished Tri-Pacer for the new mobile home which was considerably larger than the old one. As some people might say, "It's a crazy world!"

CHAPTER 8

Unscheduled Landing

Because many people have never flown in a small airplane or have never really learned much about them, much of what they do know or what they hear does not come from accurate sources and can lead to some very misleading conceptions. Probably just about every pilot has heard from a non-flying person such questions as "What do you do if the motor quits?" or "What if a wing falls off?" or "We won't crash, will we?"

Quite a few years ago, a young lady was going for a short local ride with me, her first. At the last moment as she started to walk away from the car to the plane, she decided not to take her purse and went back to put it in the car. "I'll probably never need it again anyway," she said. What confidence in the airplane and in the pilot! However, her reaction was probably like that of many who are ready for a first ride. To complete the story, she loved the ride and was ready to go again.

Not long after that, another young lady learned that I was not only a pilot but part-owner of an airplane. One of her first questions was whether or not I always wore a parachute. She seemed quite surprised when I explained that today parachutes aren't even carried in planes except military planes or for special purposes such as aerobatics.

There seems to be a general opinion that if an engine has any problem at all, the airplane will crash and all aboard are doomed or that if a plane is going down a parachute is the only answer to survival. Studies show, however, that modern airplane travel, though certainly not without accidents, is an extremely safe way to travel, even in smaller airplanes.

Undoubtedly, knowing what to do in case an emergency does arise has saved many lives. This really is a tribute to the instruction given and the willingness of the student to learn and practice necessary procedures. An emergency situation is not a normal situation by any means and, people being as they are, not every emergency is going to end up being handled just as the instructor or the manual says it should be. Too many variables are involved and in an emergency situation a pilot must do whatever is deemed best at the moment to try to bring about a safe outcome. There may not be time to reflect on exact procedure but only time for instantaneous action. On the other hand, emergencies do arise which even give the pilot time to consult the airplane manual (required to be carried on board) on what to do before final action is taken. This story may illustrate the point.

Our planned flight was just a local sightseeing jaunt in the Loveland and Greeley, Colorado, area. The flight, as it actually turned out, was not that at all! In my logbook is a column headed FROM to note where the flights originate and one headed TO, noting the place where the flights end. This day's flight shows Greeley in the FROM column but under the

TO column the note reads "irrigated field 1 mi. N. and 1 mi. E. of Greeley!"

The airplane was a rented Cessna 172 Skyhawk. Ready for takeoff from Greeley, I explained to the passengers, in order not to alarm them, that since the wind was a bit gusty, the technique for this takeoff would be a little different from the first one. The technique would be to hold the plane on the ground longer than normal, let it build a little extra speed, then lift it rather quickly to gain altitude rapidly to avoid any sudden downdrafts that might cause a problem. It is a perfectly safe technique and has been taught for years as a proper gusty-wind technique. Takeoff was absolutely normal and we were soon in a normal climb attitude, departing to the west toward the town.

Suddenly, at an altitude of only about two hundred feet, the airplane encountered a severe downdraft. It was as though a giant hand was pushing the plane toward the ground. Full power would not overcome the force and establish a positive rate of climb. We were headed down quickly and a decision had to be made in seconds.

At that low altitude, turning back toward the airport was not a good option and not even worth considering. To the left was a big field full of junked cars, trucks, and other metal in large piles. It would be a convenient place to go down only because it would save someone the trouble of hauling the airplane wreckage out there later. Convenient, yes, but not where I wanted to end up!

Straight ahead was a long row of tall and very unfriendly looking trees. We were too close to them to try to land before hitting them and carving our initials in them with the prop, wings, and other assorted pieces of the airplane. We were too low to try to go over them since the airplane would not climb, so that direction for a landing was discarded in a second. It looked like the only possibility was going to be a bright green field to the right.

There was a fence on the approach end, irrigation ditches running parallel to my landing direction and power lines at the far end. The field was not too long and from the pilot's seat, looked about half as long as it really was! But, that had to be it and a quick ninety-degree turn to the right set us up on a very short final approach.

Over the fence and into the turnips or beets or whatever they were we came. As soon as the wheels touched, I cut the power and got on the brakes. It is amazing how short a space a 172 can be landed in when one really tries! Fortunately, nobody in the airplane was hurt at all. Switches were turned off and we got out to check for damage. We had touched down a little harder than normal as the downdraft didn't seem to let up near the ground and I had the feeling of literally being driven into the ground. A Cessna's landing gear can take a lot of punishment and there was some minor damage to the gear but nothing else to my knowledge.

As we were looking at the plane and feeling very thankful that nobody was hurt, a man known locally as Skipper came running up and said he had also been caught in a downdraft earlier but apparently was just on the edge of it. He congratulated me on a good landing and, since he was one of the "old timers" at Greeley and a respected pilot who had even participated in air shows doing aerobatics, his comments were taken as quite a nice compliment.

We were given a ride back to the Fort Collins-Loveland Airport where I had rented the plane and they were told the story. Next day, one of their people went over, removed the wheel fairings, which were slightly bent, and had the airplane towed to a nearby road from which it was flown off and back to the airport with no problem.

56

I have often thought back on the incident to try to determine what could have been done to avoid the landing. The questions I have asked myself can really never be answered because I don't know exactly how things were at the time and, with everything happening in a matter of seconds, there wasn't time to worry about it. Turning another direction may have helped us fly out of the downdraft but, since air is invisible, there was no way of knowing if a turn would have improved the situation or made it worse.

All of this happened before pilots learned about what we now call a "microburst" associated with thunderstorms, which is undoubtedly what we flew into. Though there were some big cumulus clouds in the area, they did not appear to be a factor at the time. If I knew then what I know now about microbursts, the wisest choice would have been to just wait on the ground until the nasty weather had passed and the problem might never have occurred. In one sense, it was a wonderful experience because I became a better, wiser pilot in the space of a very short time! There was also the satisfaction of actually facing an emergency and handling it so that nobody aboard the airplane was hurt.

Of all the people who could have been passengers that day, the three aboard would probably be the last three I would have selected if the outcome were known ahead of time. In front, in the right seat, was my good friend, Dana Jeffries, who was very interested in flying and had just decided to start taking lessons. One purpose of the flight was to show him how fun it could be! And in the back seat, who else but my parents!

In my own mind, I am content with the decisions made in flight and the action taken. Under the circumstances, they seemed good and right. The final result was avoiding a major accident and injury to my passengers or myself and this also I attribute to good training. Many times, early in my flying, the instructor would reach over, pull the throttle back to idle while we were still quite low, and ask "Where are you going to put it?" It paid off.

I believe it would be a good idea for all pilots to determine, especially for the airports from which they fly regularly, where they would land if necessary shortly after takeoff, and not just from the most often used runway but from either end of all runways. After a while, pilots also develop the habit of watching the ground below partially to admire it's beauty and variety but also, in an almost subconscious way, to keep an eye open for a place to set the airplane down as safely as possible if necessary. Their day might come too.

CHAPTER 9

We Pause Now for a Commercial

oday, the word "commercial" is familiar to just about everyone in the country but mainly because it comes up at all sorts of inopportune times during a favorite TV program. To those who fly, the word means something else entirely. To some it means a final, long-sought-after goal, the end of long hours of training and successfully passing several required FAA tests. To others, the commercial certificate means only the beginning, the major steppingstone to a future in aviation as they pursue the ATP—the airline transport pilot certificate. It opens previously closed doors and permits access to the left seat in the airplane for pay and perhaps a lifetime career in flying. The private certificate has been compared to receiving a bachelor's degree, the commercial to receiving a master's degree, and the ATP the equivalent of a doctorate in flying.

One thing the commercial certificate does for the pilot that the private does not do is to give the privilege of flying for profit. The private pilot may be permitted to make some charges to passengers but they should be just to cover expenses and the

59

pilot must pay an equal share. The commercial certificate, by contrast, lets the pilot use learned skills and the aircraft for business as a business tool, like a company car, directly as well as indirectly related to that business. Even then, care must be taken about charging. Over the past few years, many court cases have arisen because of the fine line between what is or is not a legitimate commercial flight for which profit can be made.

Many pilots never go beyond the private certificate to the commercial and indeed really never desire or need to do so. A businessperson, for example, may use a plane simply as transportation, carrying passengers to meet business obligations. With only a private certificate, a pilot may fly both single and multi-engine aircraft, gliders, helicopters, and balloons. One may also fly on instruments in poor weather (if instrument rated) using only a private certificate and people do it many times each day.

Whatever the reason that prompts a person to go for the commercial, the route or training and the destination or privileges are the same. The requirements set forth are the same for everyone, no matter what eventual use may be made of the certificate. This is one of the bonds that unites fliers all across the country. If a pilot already holds a commercial or even an ATP and meets a new commercial pilot, the more experienced pilot knows what the other has just gone through, for he or she has done the same.

The personal stories pilots can swap about experiences peculiar to their training sessions make for some interesting listening around the lounge on a winter day when the only thing flying is the slightly exaggerated versions of these training flights or other aerial adventures. A private pilot often looks up to the commercially rated ones and often sees them as a source of learning more about the art of flying. Often, the more experienced pilots may even become mentors to the fledglings.

This bond is probably much like that which unites members of other groups. The requirements may be written, formal declarations such as those outlined by the FAA for the commercial or they may be only in the form of an understanding as determined by the people in the group itself. Everyone at some time is, has been or will be, no doubt, a member of such a group.

An example is our thirteen-year-old daughter, Joy, who was in a group of youngsters learning to ride horses for several summers. She looked up to those with more riding skills and learned from them as well as from the instructors. She is now in a group learning karate and, as an intermediate student, admires those wearing advanced belts and looks forward to the day when she will be wearing one and helping less experienced students learn the basics. She learns from watching those with the advanced belts just as pilots learn from one another. In any society, or in a small part of a society, there is a kindred spirit which others—the "outsiders"—do not fully understand.

By way of another illustration, imagine a young boy at a swimming pool standing on the highest diving board for his first time. Below, a group of friends who have already made the dive wait for him to make that same plunge. There has been no special training and no requirements are written down about making the dive, but to be one of the "elite," to be one who has made it, he must pass the same test others before him have passed. Of course there are only two choices, to dive and not to dive. To choose not to dive should not make the boy an outcast, a "sissy," or a failure. He may have talents that the other boys do not possess. Each person should be considered as an individual and given credit for what he or she can do rather than be criticized for what he or she cannot do. Unfortunately, both children and adults are far too ready to criticize than to praise. The boy then must choose whether it is worthwhile to him as a person to make the plunge into the unknown.

We all face such decisions in life to various extents. We may, in some situations, seek advice as to whether a particular goal is really what we should pursue. With as much information gathered as we can get or care to get, a decision is made but each person must decide in his or her own mind whether a goal is worth whatever is involved to reach it.

Facing the possibility of changing jobs probably happens to thousands of people each day and many factors must be considered. There are considerations not only of pay but also of location, change of home perhaps, and even giving up some friends to make new ones. The type of people with whom one will associate in a new job, the pressures involved, perhaps change in responsibility, and other factors must be weighed. Finally, like the boy on the high diving board, a decision is made to dive, to take the plunge, or not. For some, the choice is simple and quick but for others it may take time, maybe an agonizingly long time to decide what to do.

In choosing whether to work or not to work toward a commercial certificate, a pilot also is faced with factors to weigh. Will it benefit me? How? Does my type of flying justify the time and expense involved? Can my bank account afford it without putting me in poverty for longer than I care to be there? How would this affect my family?

Deciding not to continue beyond the private level should not make one less of a pilot in the eyes of others. Indeed, there are many private pilots whose knowledge, skill, safety precautions, care of an aircraft, sense of responsibility, etc., make them far better pilots than some commercial pilots who manage to obtain the certificate but quickly forget, or choose not to use, the information accumulated in the additional training involved for the higher skill level. Personally, I would rather be a passenger with the wiser, safer, private pilot.

My own personal reasons for obtaining a commercial certificate were varied. For one, I saw it as a highly regarded accomplishment and I wanted to see if I could reach that goal just for my own satisfaction. Also, flying instruction wasn't getting any cheaper so waiting to obtain the certificate would be even more expensive. Further, I already had the minimum flying time so a lot of the requirements had been met. Requirements change over the years too and as long as I had the hours, it seemed reasonable to start the process now before the requirements got stiffer and the cost to meet them would go up at the same time. Finally, it was simply something I wanted to do and had a opportunity to do, to "strike while the iron is hot," so to speak.

Perhaps you can recall a time, when you had a chance to do something you really desired to do but for some reason found an excuse not to carry the plan through. You thought that maybe another time would be better and then later found it not possible and regretted passing up the opportunity. Life is full of wasted opportunities and I have certainly passed up many that I regretted later. At the same time, many of the best times in my life resulted from taking advantage of opportunities when they presented themselves. To pass them up would have been a mistake. Taking the chances have made life far more rewarding.

Even the publishing of this book would serve as a good example. The manuscript had been written for quite a long time but nothing was done with it. Then the day came to make a decision to do it, to take the plunge from the high diving board into the unknown water of writing and publishing. Yes, there were risks. Writing was not the only difficult task; marketing the book would take as much effort, if not more.

But there was also the possibility of reward for the effort put forth, part of which could be monetary but part could also be the satisfaction of carrying the project through from concept to finished product.

Jim Lafferty was a fairly new CFI (certified flight instructor) at the Fort Collins Downtown Airport where I was flying at the time and he was to be my instructor for the commercial certificate. Jim was a friendly guy with many qualities one should look for in an instructor, including a generous portion of patience.

The plane we used was a 1966 Cessna 150, N8523G, which my friend, Dana, and I had purchased just two months earlier. It had been used as an instrument trainer and was well equipped for a 150; in addition to the basic instruments, it also had a glide slope indicator, marker beacon, and pitot heat.

At the time my private certificate was issued no instrument flight training was required for it as it is now. The requirements for the commercial included at least ten hours of flight with reference to instruments only. That part was not difficult, in fact, it was enjoyable and I worked hard at it. Many of the maneuvers for the commercial are about the same as for the private but the area of acceptable error is smaller—altitudes and compass headings, for example, need to be more precise.

The instrument work was also good preparation for the instrument rating later. Lessons included flying while using both the full panel of instruments and practice with some of the instruments covered as if unusable. Instructors seem to make partial panel work one of their favorite games. Pilots across the country have probably sensed the evil smirk that comes across the instructor's face as he or she covers one instrument after another. Or they have sensed the glee with which instructors watch a student's knuckles whiten on the controls and beads of sweat appear from under the student's visibility-restricting visor as the airplane is flown using only minimum instruments.

Takeoffs and landings of all sorts were practiced—normal, short field, soft field, over a fifty-foot obstacle, with and without flaps, and aborted ones.

The review was excellent. It is too easy just to jump into an airplane, crank it up, and take off to go from point A to point B, paying little attention to holding predetermined altitudes, headings, and speeds, then finally completing the trip by making something only remotely resembling a descent landing. Too much of that sort of flying gets to be habit after a while and many of the safe and correct techniques may not be at hand if the occasion should arise to need them. Airplanes are pretty forgiving machines up to a point, but the point isn't always very far away and if the airplane gets ahead of the pilot instead of the pilot mentally being ahead of the plane, things can go sour faster than unrefrigerated milk.

The written, or knowledge test, was already out of the way. I had chosen to study for it at home instead of taking a ground school course and passed on the first attempt. Any pilot from a number of years B.C. (before computers) who has taken a written FAA exam for any certificate or rating knows the feeling of waiting for the test results. Because tests are now given on a computer, the results are known within a few minutes of finishing.

In the past, the test was sent to FAA headquarters in Oklahoma City by mail and one had to wait a couple of weeks or more for the scores to come by return mail. Opening the envelope to see the results was akin to opening the envelopes at the Oscar or Emmy awards program when the master of ceremonies says, "May I have the envelope, please?" I have walked out of FAA testing rooms feeling I had really aced a test only to find out later that the score was acceptable but not always something to write home about. It is also a sober-ing thought to realize that one can successfully pass an FAA exam with a score of only 70 percent. That means it is legal to fly without really knowing 30 percent of the material! One advantage to the three-step testing system, however, is that the examiner who gives the oral test usually has your knowl-edge exam results and can cover more thoroughly the areas in which you were weak. They can sometimes be checked again during the flight test.

A gentleman by the name of Lloyd Lair was to give the oral and flight tests. The flight time to get ready was spread over five weeks, and the logbook was signed by Jim on September 16 to say I was ready. (He either signed because he really felt I was ready or because he had had all he could stand, hope-fully the former.) Truthfully, I felt well prepared and give Jim a lot of credit for his instruction. It was another week before Lloyd and I could get together for the testing and I did not get back in the air for any last-minute practice, though it probably would have been a good thing to do.

Both the oral and flight tests went well. Lloyd was a big man and the plane was right up to gross weight for takeoff. Occasionally an examiner will have a student do a maneuver differently than the way the student learned it and this is re-ally not unusual. Once or twice Lloyd demonstrated a certain maneuver the way he wanted it done and it was a pleasure to watch him fly. He flew as easily and relaxed as he looked and spoke and moved on the ground—efficient but not in a big rush. Often he smoked a pipe and, when flying, he looked so relaxed I almost expected him to take it out of his pocket and light up in the middle of a chandelle or lazy eight.

Like CFIs, examiners must spend hours practicing certain things that all of them have in common. Apparently, they all take ground school courses in subjects such as Lack of Facial

Expressions 101 or Silent Treatment 204 because during the flight tests you usually don't get a clue from the examiner's face or voice as to how well or how poorly you are doing.

After a one-hour forty-minute ride that included about every maneuver learned in practice, we landed and shut down the engine. I don't recall hearing a word from Lloyd until after he finished making out the temporary certificate. But then he had his big grin and open manner back; that was his way, he was always a good man—demanding but fair. During the drive home as probably the newest commercial pilot in the country at the moment, the sun seemed a little brighter, the sky a little bluer and I was a very happy guy! Nobody did the final test for me, I did it on my own—I had dived off the high board and joined a slightly different group. Of course, many people helped and encouraged me on the way, for which I remain very grateful.

Maybe not everything had been done 100 percent right but I knew I had done a good job and felt a right to hold my head just a bit higher, not to get my nose higher in the air, you understand, but because of a good sense of accomplishment. A risk had been taken, the goal had been attained, and life was just a little nicer.

Just so, in your own life, when opportunities present themselves to you, don't be too anxious to reject them. There will be pros and cons to consider but you should also listen with your heart and not only with your mind. If you are not ready for the giant economy-sized risks, try some very small ones first. Do what you are comfortable with. I am not completely endorsing the "if it feels good, do it" philosophy but within limits, within your own personal ethics and morals, the good feeling about something may be the nudge you need to step out and try something new or different in your life. I hope you will try it and that you'll be happy you did.

CHAPTER 10

*T*he Cessna 150 was, and still is, one of the smaller trainer aircraft built. It has only two seats, a fairly small engine, and a small cabin: two people are very cozy in it unless they are both quite small. Still, it does give one wings, is relatively inexpensive to own and to operate, and can fly into and out of probably just about any airport in the country. It certainly is not fast but if it is being used as a time builder, being a little slow can be an advantage. If one has the time and some patience, there is no reason it cannot be flown anywhere in the country. The two wing tanks hold only twenty-six gallons of fuel but it doesn't drink that fuel in large gulps as many larger planes do; it sips it at a more affordable rate per hour. There are still many used ones on the market, but they are definitely beginning to show their age unless extremely well maintained.

Dana and I did a lot of looking and considered a number of different types before settling on the 150 we bought. There is a great deal to take into consideration, a lot to look at, and a lot to look for when beating the bushes for a good used plane. Some research is always a good idea for things to be careful of in general and things to watch for specifically on any plane. We took our time and felt we finally made a good buy when the time came to lay the money on the table. Within a week after buying N8523G, the three-hundredth hour was logged in my book. It was good to have wings again and neither Dana nor I let it get rusty from lack of use.

Less than a month after signing the ownership papers, an opportunity came about to try out our new (to us) machine on a nice cross-country trip. A friend of mine, Leon Atkins, from my hometown, needed to go to Texas and I was glad to have a chance to give the bird a good cross-country trial.

We really did not get off to a great start, though, because the way I needed to go and the way the wind wanted to blow were just about 180 degrees out of sync. Picking up my passenger at our hometown of Haxtun, I set a southeast course toward Goodland, Kansas. Battling a direct headwind of around thirty knots, we flashed over the ground at a blazing sixty-three mph, barely keeping up with the ground traffic below. It did ease up later but, since we started rather late, we decided to overnight in Scott City, Kansas. Still, even at that speed, because we were going southeast and the roads nearly all run north-south or east-west in that part of the country, we made the trip much faster than could be done by car. A car would have a much slower average speed and have to cover more miles to the same destination.

Much of Oklahoma is very pretty to fly over and one thing that makes it so is the very red color of the soil and the beautiful blue of the sky. At least from a Cessna 150 one can really enjoy the scenery because low and slow is often the name of the game.

All in all, it did turn out to be a good trip. It added a little over seventeen hours to the logbook by the time the bird was back in Fort Collins and 23G had performed well all the way. I had the feeling that we had made a good purchase.

Every now and then there is a story in the paper or in one of the aviation magazines about some pilot with more gold on his sleeve than most of us have in the bank and more hours in his logbook than most pilots will ever see, who does something so silly—like landing an airliner full of passengers at the wrong airport (it has happened) that it should be a reminder to the weekend pilots in their little two-or four-place jobs not to get uptight if, now and then, they also make some blunder on a flight, as long as it is not the result of recklessness or foolhardiness. Most pilots probably try to make each flight a model one but they seldom turn out to be 100 percent perfect.

There is one flight logged in my books that will never be forgotten and could rank up with the best of them when stories are swapped at the local airport. All it took was the little Cessna 150 and a combination of events falling together to form a ridiculous and rather embarrassing tale. But I enjoy laughing at myself sometimes and so pass the incident along with the idea that it might help somebody else along the way. It was only three months after obtaining the commercial certificate that this took place, which probably made it a bit more embarrassing! That ticket meant I should be able to find my way from A to B reasonably well and in a safe, efficient, and professional manner.

Christmas vacation was approaching and I suggested to a good friend from Fort Collins, Tim Kessler, that we head for the warmer clime of San Antonio to hit a few golf balls. Tim was quite a golfing enthusiast at the time so it didn't take much to persuade him to join up. Early in the morning on December 18 we stowed our suitcases, golf clubs, maps, and all the other odds and ends one usually can find, into the back of the Cessna. So far, the trip was going great!

The first planned fuel stop was at Lamar, Colorado. Since the 150 is comparatively slow and sometimes agonizingly so on a trip and because it doesn't hold much fuel, a second stop was made at Canadian, Texas. Nobody was around the tiny airport when we arrived but it was close to noon so we waited a short while, figuring they had slipped into town for a bite of lunch. Finally, we decided to move on but ran into stronger headwinds than we had figured on and landed at Sayre, Oklahoma, with the fuel gauges moving toward the low end. The end of a very short winter day found us at Brownwood, Texas. Being unfamiliar with the countryside, I decided not to push on at night so we called it enough for one day. Besides, one cannot sightsee much at night.

Next morning we took off and pointed 8523G toward San Antonio, but you know what they say about the best laid plans of mice and men . . . .. Texas is an awfully big piece of real estate to cross, even in an airplane, and much of it is not too inviting for either driving or flying. There are parts of Texas that can best be described as just miles and miles of miles and miles.

The last VOR navigation station we passed was about out of receiving range behind us but so far I had been unable to pick up a signal from the next one ahead that was needed and there was not another one handy for a short detour. They sometimes are terribly far apart at the wrong time! A while later, a radio call to another station confirmed my suspicions—the station we needed was temporarily shut down for repair. No real problem—all that was necessary to do was hold an accurate compass course to the next checkpoint. The idea was simple enough but now another small item crept in to add to the situation.

We had been flying fairly low and I could not pick up other VOR signals ahead. The next decision was to simply climb to a higher altitude to see if reception could be improved for another station further south. Sounds good, right? Another small problem arose—clouds. They were quite solid ahead but were mostly lower, stratus types. Before long we reached the edge of the cloudbank and went on over the top, remaining VFR with excellent visibility. Since I was not IFR rated at the time and did not want to get caught on top of a solid under-cast, my choice was to continue south above the clouds for a short while. Later, if they looked like they would remain solid underneath, we would turn east until reaching the edge of the cloud bank, which I still had in sight, and go back underneath. You guessed it—no holes showed up so I dropped the left wing and headed east.

By now, my position was not terribly accurate. Well, the position itself was accurate enough, the thing was, I was not exactly sure where that position was. I certainly did not con-sider us lost at all because I had a good idea generally where we were; it was just difficult to pin it down to a fine point. Not having seen a checkpoint or anything useable for some time, and not knowing how far the wind might have blown us off course, I could only make an estimate of our position.

Shortly, we were back at the edge of the undercast so we dropped back under the clouds and once again headed south. Tim was watching the map, or at least trying to, the air was getting rougher, and we were bouncing around like a rubber ball. By now the clouds and the ground were getting much friendlier and we were forced down lower to remain legal. According to the map, there should be a major highway run-ning east and west not far ahead if we were anywhere close to where we thought so I held the same course south. About ten minutes later our highway came into view straight ahead. Not knowing at what point we intercepted the highway, I decided to turn west since I had earlier flown east to get back below the clouds. The way I reasoned, we should be back close to our original course in another ten or fifteen minutes.

We bounced along, following the highway, looking for something on which to get a bearing. With the visibility down to just a few miles under the clouds, location of a town, lake, or some other good checkpoint more than a short distance away was impossible and I didn't want to wander away from the highway looking for something I might not find. The highway would eventually bring us to a town we could identify, but a lot of Texas towns are a long way apart.

Then Tim called out that he saw a runway just ahead on the right, near the highway! I was busy trying to keep the airplane more or less level so just glanced at the map he was holding, but neither of us could identify it right then. There was no town nearby and rather than fly on and risk running out of fuel, it seemed as good a place as any to set down, get fuel, and get squared away as to just where we were. A few seconds later we were on downwind then base and then on final approach.

Just before we were ready to land, we noticed the word "PRIVATE" painted across the end of the runway. The situation we were in was not really desperate, but then it was not comfortable either with the weather down, fuel getting low, turbulence, and an unknown exact position, so the decision was to go ahead and land.

As we neared the taxiway on down the runway, Tim made a comment about the fancy cars near the buildings. We also noticed a nice twin-engine Beechcraft parked nearby. With the engine shut down, we got out to get ourselves located and see about some fuel. We also noticed a lot of antennas on top of the buildings and got the feeling that this wasn't your everyday ranch strip out in the boondocks. At one of the buildings our knock was answered by a man in uniform and I'm not sure who was more surprised, him or us.

"Did you just land here?" he asked, rather sharply.

I said that we had and explained very briefly our situation, including the fact that we had not very much fuel remaining and that it seemed better to land here than to run out of gas out in the sagebrush somewhere.

"I don't care if you get killed somewhere else," he said rather roughly, "but if you'd get killed here I'd have a lot of paperwork to fill out on you!"

After that warm, friendly greeting, the gentleman calmed down a bit and walked over to the plane where he took our names and the number of the plane down in a notebook. We had been getting some hints as to where we were but when he pointed out the place on the map, were we ever surprised! Out of all the airports in the whole state of Texas, I had just landed smack on Lyndon B. Johnson's ranch, and at the time he was President of the United States! No wonder the guard had been upset! Apparently, we had been flying so low for so long, we had come in under the radar surveillance and had not been spotted on the screen.

As it turned out, I really couldn't blame the guard for being upset because I can see how anybody could land there and claim some false reason for having to do so, just to say that they had done it, or even to cause trouble. Certainly I would not advocate other people doing something like that—they might not get off as easily as we did.

When the guard pointed out our position on the map, I was also pleasantly surprised to find out something else. Upon landing, we couldn't have been more on course if there had been a line drawn on the ground to follow; my red course line on the map crossed directly through the airport we were on! A quick check showed we had sufficient fuel to reach an airport just on the outskirts of San Antonio where we chose to stay. By this time the weather had improved slightly and looked better further south so we moved on. We had probably already worn out our welcome anyway!

The golfing was enjoyable, the weather was beautiful, and we spent a delightful few days relaxing and seeing a few of the sights including the famous Alamo. The return trip was fine but a bit anticlimactic after the experiences on the way south. Word managed to get around the local airport back home and it took a while to live down the greetings as I would walk in and be welcomed with something like "Hi, Jim. What do you hear from your buddy Lyndon today?"

CHAPTER 11

Delivery Pilot

$\mathcal{A}$bright, shiny new airplane rolling up to a stop in front of the terminal, perhaps one just parked on the flight line, maybe one taxiing out for takeoff, or flashing by on departure are nearly always sights that draw someone's attention at an airport. It makes little difference whether the airport is a large metropolitan one or a small rural airstrip. The size of the airplane often doesn't matter so much either; some people watch the small ones with the same attention the bigger ones receive.

Even the smallest airports seem to occasionally have one or two new planes around, maybe privately owned and sometimes to demonstrate for sale. In the summer of 1974, I found out how a lot of those planes reach their destinations from the factories where they are built. Or, maybe it would be better said that I finally became more aware of it than before because it was then that an opportunity came along to do some delivery flights (or ferry flights as they are sometimes called). I prefer to be called a "delivery pilot" because it's not so easy to misinterpret as it is if someone uses the term "ferry pilot" and thinks of the word "ferry" with a different spelling.

It came about when I was looking through the *Trade-A-Plane* paper one day and noticed an ad that intrigued me. Someone was advertising a need for a pilot with at least a thousand hours' flight time, experience flying cross-country with no radios, and with taildragger experience. It did not say exactly what the job was but it gave a phone number, somewhere back East. At that time, my logbook showed only seven hundred hours but I did meet the other qualifications so I made a call.

It turned out that a delivery company in Lock Haven, Pennsylvania, where Piper had a factory at the time, needed pilots to fly new planes to various places in the country to their new owners. Most of those to be delivered were small, single-engine craft.

The man speaking to me, Hank Koenig, of the Ferry Service Company, explained that a new Piper Pawnee spray plane needed to go to Nogales, Arizona, for final delivery later to Mexico. As I heard on the phone the type of airplane it was and considered the distance and the fact that there was no radio, thoughts raced through my mind as to whether I should accept the trip or not. Hank had told me by this time that he would take me with the seven hundred hours. One minor little detail that also crossed my mind was that I had seen a Pawnee before but had probably never even looked inside one, let alone flown one. Hank finished giving the basic facts about the trip and, not totally sure of what I was getting into, my answer was, "Okay, I'll take it!"

More thoughts ran through my mind after the conversation was finished. The Pawnee is a crop duster and spray plane with only one seat, so there could be no dual instruction given in it before departing on the trip. It is also a taildragger and it had been quite a while since I had flown one. Further, this would not be a one-takeoff, one-landing flight. Pennsylvania to Arizona is a long trip, even in a jet. In a Pawnee it is a very, very, long flight with many takeoffs and landings. The thought of piling up somebody else's brand new airplane during either takeoff or landing wasn't pleasant so I tried to concentrate on the good side of such a flight that was to be made in just the next couple of days. It sounded like a challenge and a neat way to see more of the United States from the air so, immediately, preparations were under way. Because it was during the summer break and because I was not married, the freedom to pick up and leave for a week or more on a moment's notice was not a problem.

Now that the decision had been made, I felt that I could do the job and do it well. Within about three hours, laundry was done, mail pickup arrangements made, traveler's checks purchased, a plane ticket to Pennsylvania ordered, a couple of phone calls were made, maps laid out, the computer, logbook, flashlight, and a few other things organized. Everything was packed into one small suitcase and I was aboard the bus headed for Denver for the flight to Pennsylvania.

Travel has always been a favorite part of my life, whether in the United States or abroad, so I welcomed the opportunity to visit the East just for a mini vacation as well as to make the flight. A combination of buses, airplane, and taxi finally brought me into Lock Haven late at night so a room was obtained at a local hotel and I waited to see what the following day would bring.

It brought fog! Lock Haven sits in a nice valley along the Susquehanna River and the whole scene is quite peaceful for the amount of activity going on there. Summer mornings in Colorado usually dawn bright and clear. Fog is a rarity and, what little there is usually burns off quickly. Because of the higher humidity in the East, fog is much more common and when it comes, it doesn't kid around. It is often thick and may not burn off all day long. And if it isn't foggy, it is hazy much of the time, at least such was the case each time I was there. (Once I went in March and the sky was so blue one morning, I thought I had gotten off the bus in the wrong state!) The haze may extend several thousand feet up from the surface and cover a number of states.

Piper's airport was just at the edge of town, so I walked the mile or so from the hotel and had a chance to see a bit of the town on the way. At the Ferry Service Company office, I met Hank for the first time in person, a friendly fellow with a ready smile. He wanted to get the airplane on the way as soon as possible but was also concerned about the safety of his pilots, which I appreciated. Right then, the weather was poor and he did not pressure me to leave. Of course, the weather probably looked much worse to me than to him and I wasn't anxious to go charging off into the wild gray yonder until the odds looked more in my favor. The Ferry Service Company had printouts of weather information available right there so making a "go" or "no-go" decision was not difficult.

Still waiting for the weather to improve, Hank gave me the required paperwork and also showed me on a large U.S. map several places along the route where fuel could be purchased at the lowest prices. I also got the manual from the airplane's papers and sat down to find out just what to do with this strange bird. Later, Hank pointed out various features of the plane and certain things to look for during the preflight inspection. Time went slowly, probably because of being anxious to get under way. The plane had been fueled and the suitcase stored in the hopper where the chemical is usually placed since there is no other available space. The Pawnee is made for a specific job and it certainly is not made for a cross-country trip in luxury.

Also, I had given the plane an extra-careful preflight check since it was brand-new. The workmen who built it no doubt knew their job but workers are human and can make mistakes. It's a whole lot easier to discover something wrong and correct it on the ground than to discover a problem in the air and try to correct it then. On one new plane I was to deliver, three of the four latches used to secure the top half of the engine cowling were not properly secured at all. Had that not been noticed during the preflight inspection, half the cowling might have come off in flight—that could ruin my whole afternoon!

The flight plan was ready to file so, until departure time came, most of the time was spent looking at other planes, reading magazines, and rereading the Pawnee manual. Finally, about three p.m., the weather had cleared enough to go so the flight plan was filed and I climbed aboard, little realizing how much time we would be spending together, low and slow and hot and loud! Even getting into the airplane was a new experience and there is a graceful way to do it and many awkward ways. Hank explained the easiest way was to stand on the wing facing aft and, with the left hand, grasp the top of the windshield or the bar extending down the center of the windshield (later, I learned this sharpened bar was a wire deflector and cutter in case power lines try to snag the airplane during dusting or spraying operations). The left foot is placed inside first and finally you pivot and bring in the right foot. I was in; so far I was handling the plane quite well.

The seat of the Pawnee is quite comfortable and for that I was thankful during the long hours. Visibility is very good, though slight S-turns make seeing things close in front of the long nose easier. There wasn't much to check before takeoff because the instrument panel is the extreme in simplicity, almost like the old T-Craft of student pilot days. Fuel quantity, oil pressure, compass (magnetic), and altimeter were checked and the engine run up to check the magnetos. It seemed strange to see only 0.4 hours on the engine. The shoulder harness was locked, the door secured, and TEX and I were ready to go. Since the airplane was of Mexican registration, it did not carry the familiar U.S. numbers or letters but was designated XB-TEX..

Looking around the cockpit, I couldn't help but be amused by a thought about the lever that opened the door of the hopper under the airplane to release the chemical dust normally housed there but which now contained my suitcase. What if a guy pulled that lever instead of the lever to lower the flaps and sent the contents of the suitcase sprawling all over some farmer's field in the middle of Indiana or in a river, or in the middle of main street in Anytown, U.S.A.?

Lined up in the center of the runway, I eased the throttle forward and learned a new lesson very quickly. About the time I thought the joystick should be moved forward a bit to raise the tail, the plane was already ten feet in the air! With only one small suitcase in the hopper instead of a full load of chemical, the plane was very light and literally jumped off the ground. Later takeoffs were more as they should be. The fuel tanks held only thirty-six gallons, enough for about three hours. Usually, a leg of the trip would be planned for about two hours and twenty or thirty minutes to allow for reserve. With a new engine and no trial record to see how much it would actually burn per hour, it seemed prudent to leave more than the required half-hour reserve in the tanks.

I was not familiar at all with the Pennsylvania countryside so the plan was to first fly south down the valley until picking up Interstate 80 going west. Visibility was poor at best but following the Interstate made the job much easier. Due to the haze, any town, lake, or any other descent checkpoint would have been useless if more than about three miles to either side.

82

With no radio, the wisest choice seemed to be just to hang on to the ribbon of highway unless it seemed possible to deviate from it with a good amount of assurance that needed checkpoints could not be missed without some gross navigational error. Experience is very valuable and much was gained on this and later trips. For example, on one trip, I noticed how the fog clung to the bottom of every small valley and while most of the countryside was visible, nearly every small town was hidden from view by its blanket of fog. Trying to use them as checkpoints in those conditions was out of the question.

The first landing in the Pawnee was really not a problem, but I had received some good advice before leaving Lock Haven on what to watch for. The long nose of that plane has quite a pronounced downward slant to it and when the plane is in level flight, it appears that one is already in a fairly good descent attitude. Watching the angle of the wing tips relative to the horizon was an easy way to maintain level flight without reference to any instruments. On final approach, with the nose down where it belongs, there is, at first, the impression it is going to dive right into the ground. Keeping in mind where the nose actually belongs is a big help and as I bounced across the U.S. in short hops over the next few days, there was plenty of opportunity to try some different techniques and iron out some of the rough spots related to making good landings.

The entire trip from Lock Haven to Nogales took twenty-five flying hours. Going west, one normally expects some headwinds and they held true to form, giving a ground speed of about 85 or 90 mph. At only about two and a half hours between fuel stops, there were lots of chances to meet and talk with people along the way, but then that was part of the fun. There was also a lot of time to really take in the vast variety and beauty of our country. Seeing it from only a few hundred feet up is much different than seeing the same thing from a car or from a jet at thirty thousand feet and six hundred miles an hour. Just to watch the landscape unfold and change was a vacation in itself. Of course, having no radio and navigating just by watching and constantly comparing ground and map, I probably got more out of the scenery than most pilots who tune in a VOR and follow the needle while really giving only an occasional glance at the land below.

Overall, the trip was delightful. Many might take exception to that statement if flying to them means doing it at high altitude in living room comfort and relative quiet, watching a movie or listening to music en route as a passenger. As a pilot, flying might mean always being surrounded with many electronic goodies to help navigate and communicate. Don't get me wrong—I certainly enjoy the same things but this was a chance to make a long trip the way few people can. I found enjoyment in the noise of the engine, the rush of the wind, the smell of new fabric, the skills needed to navigate on only basic instruments, the freedom of being alone with the airplane, and the sense of accomplishment to deliver the airplane in good condition to the new owner.

Later, after delivering XB-TEX and settled down in a Greyhound bus (sometimes faster than the Pawnee in a headwind) back toward Colorado, there was time for more reflection. It was pleasant to think about the people, the new towns, the airports that were no longer just names on a map, the rolling Pennsylvania hills, the green farmlands of Ohio and Indiana, the mighty Mississippi River with its never-ending barges shuffling back and forth, the plains of Kansas and Oklahoma, and the desolate desert areas of Texas and Arizona. I was pleasantly tired because the job I wanted to do well had been done, and done well indeed.

CHAPTER 12

More Deliveries

One month after delivering XB-TEX to Nogales, Arizona, another call came from Hank at the Ferry Service Company to deliver another Pawnee (XB-KOY) and, interesting enough, it was to go to the same destination and to the same new owner. One distinct advantage of being a teacher was having some free time in the summer to do this kind of work (if you can call it work). Many people would probably love to do something different from their daily jobs but are too tied to their work to be very flexible.

Generally, it would take about a week to make a fairly long trip. Allowing two days' travel to the factory by bus and one or two to get home again, and from two to four days of flying plus a day or two extra thrown in to allow for layovers due to weather quickly used up six or seven days.

For most travel to the factory and home again, the bus was used simply to save money over airfare. By taking a few sandwiches, sleeping on the bus for two nights and sometimes staying overnight with a friend or relative along the way, I could just break even or maybe make a dollar or two on each trip. Usually, pay received for such flights was so little, it would just barely cover minimum expenses. I had so much fun doing it though, that I would have almost paid them to let me fly.

That is the way anyone's lifetime work should be—finding something you enjoy doing so much that you would be willing to pay someone else to let you do it. Perhaps this is where the idea of making a change in a career by being willing to take a bit of a risk, to dive from the high diving board, comes into play if it really feels like the thing your heart tells you to do.

The second trip to Nogales was much like the first but the airplane was now more familiar and, with some experience under my (seat) belt the flying, navigating, and other details came somewhat easier. As mentioned above, sometimes flights could be planned that would allow visits to friends and relatives seldom seen. With relatives scattered around the country, visits by car did not happen often, but on a long trip such as this, deviating slightly from a straight-line course is hardly noticeable and it added to the pleasure of the trip; it sort of put the airplane in the "magic carpet" category. But, at the same time, as a pilot with a responsibility to bring the airplane to the new owner without undue delay, often opportunities were passed up to stop and visit some famous or just interesting place along the way.

Each trip was, first of all, a business to be carried out to satisfy the customer. A flight was not a real vacation in the sense that the pilot could deviate all over the country sightseeing and take his own sweet time—that was not what the delivery business was about. There was also a reputation to be earned with the Ferry Service Company as a reliable and trustworthy pilot. Not doing the job right would almost certainly result in not being called for any future flights, and that would be the right thing to happen.

Just a week after XB-KOY was delivered, I received a third call from Lock Haven for a trip to Greenville, Mississippi. It looked like it was going to be a busy summer and I couldn't think of a better way to spend it. This time the airplane to be flown was a Piper Super Cub. Super Cubs have been around for many years and are still used a great deal. I had never had a chance to fly one but was extremely interested so, again, in just a few hours the small suitcase was packed, all details taken care of at home and I was another Greyhound passenger headed east. I'm quite sure more time was spent riding in buses that summer than was spent in flight and the main problem was that the bus hours could not be written up in the pilot's log as part of the flights!

Another good lesson was to be learned from this trip and perhaps it will help another pilot along the way. I open myself up to a lot of kidding from stories like this but can laugh at myself and enjoy it as well so there is no problem. This is the flight related back in chapter 5 where I became "slightly misplaced" for a while due to a magnetic compass that was not properly adjusted when installed in the airplane. Once the problem was fixed, the flight continued without further incident to Greenville. It was my first time flying down in the Deep South and it was fascinating to see how much different the landscape seemed there compared to other areas of the country.

It was particularly thrilling to dip down low over the Mississippi River with its many barges strung out like chains and wave at them by wagging the wings back and forth and then seeing the barge crew wave a greeting in reply. Fellow travelers, fellow adventurers, passing for only a moment then going our own separate ways. It is sort of like motorcycle riders who traditionally lift their left hand in greeting to other bikers out on the highway. A sort of kinship of free spirits exists among those who are members of that particular group, even though they may never speak to or see each other again. Car drivers, do not wave at each other (unless both are special, like the Corvette) just because they both drive cars—cars are too common.

The Piper company also had a factory in Florida at Vero Beach, where it continues to manufacture aircraft today under its title of The New Piper Aircraft Corporation. Vero Beach sits right on the Atlantic and is quite a change of scenery from Lock Haven and certainly from Colorado. My contact for the Ferry Service Company in Vero Beach was Bill Sparks. It was he who phoned me in the summer of 1975 and asked if I was interested in flying a new Cherokee 140 from Vero Beach to the new owners in Teterboro, New Jersey, just across the river from New York City. Was I interested? Do kids like ice cream? Holding the phone with one hand, I was already throwing things in the well-traveled little brown suitcase with the other!

Even though the Cherokee was just a small airplane, often used as a trainer, it was nice to get a job flying it after the Pawnees and the Super Cub. In a way, it's difficult to say which type of plane was the more enjoyable to fly. There was something about the Pawnees that was almost enticing. Maybe it was because it was such a basic airplane, just bare bones and a taildragger to boot. Maybe it was partly because it is a type of plane relatively few pilots ever have a chance to fly. Certainly the Cherokee was more comfortable and the equipment included not only a radio with a VOR but also a transponder. This was really a change! A little bit of Cherokee 140 time was already in the logbook and since my own plane at the time was a Cherokee 180, there was certainly no problem getting accustomed to it. Just a couple of times around the patch with Bill and I was ready to take N1442X north.

The uniqueness of this trip was that I had never flown up the Atlantic coast before and never in the New York City area. A lot of tales had been spread about the New York area and how the sky is full of flying metal. Stories abounded about the unfriendliness of ground controllers there as well. Maybe there is some truth to the stories but if this trip was normal at all, the stories are greatly exaggerated.

Takeoff from Vero Beach was much later than anticipated and the end of the day found 42X and me only as far north as Rocky Mount, North Carolina. The following day, the route north went through the Washington, D.C., area, which was really quite simple. Remember, this was 1975 and the regulations and traffic were not as complex as today. The people with whom I was in radio contact on the ground were pleasant even though they were not talking to a Boeing 747. A brief stop was made in Gaithersburg, Maryland (this time I landed in Maryland intentionally) to try to visit my brother, Bob, who was working then in Washington for the National Park Service. Office duties prevented him from being free, however, so the plane was refueled, as was my stomach, and I moved on, hoping to arrive in Teterboro before the people at the destination, New York Piper Sales, left for the day.

Approaching from the south, I radioed a position report over Colt's Neck VOR and was soon in radio contact with the gentleman who would direct the final few miles of the trip into the New York area. Upon initial radio contact, besides giving position, altitude, heading, type of aircraft. and destination, I also explained that this was my first time to the New York area and I was not familiar with it. He was great! He was not handling a Lear jet or some other exotic bird but he was as polite and helpful as if he were handling some celebrity's flight.

A new altitude was suggested and the Verrazano Bridge was given as the next reporting point. He explained where to look for the Statue of Liberty and what a sight it was to see Lady Liberty's torch lifted to the sky, almost like a personal welcome! Following the Hudson River, I was kept at a very low altitude and had to look up to see the tops of skyscrapers only a short distance away at the edge of the river. It was a tremendous and unique experience!

Soon, 42X was turned over to Teterboro tower for landing instructions and the flight was concluded much more easily than some trips I've made into far smaller and less busy places. Since the September 11 tragedy, New York is much more restricted so it was a pleasure to be able to make the flight when the opportunity was there.

Immediately after delivering the 140, I placed a call to Lock Haven, since I was already so close to Pennsylvania to see if there might possibly be another flight to be picked up. Sure enough, Hank had a new Pawnee Brave ready to go to Hayti, Missouri, which is right on the Mississippi River not far from Memphis. Putting two flights together without returning to Colorado first was fortunate because it would save a lot of money and time which meant, with a little good fortune, perhaps there would actually be a little cash left over after the delivery to Missouri. Soon I was on another bus going back to Lock Haven.

This time the airplane, N9952P, was going to Mid-Continent Aircraft Corporation. It differed slightly from the other Pawnees delivered earlier in that it used the newer Tiara engine and swung a three-bladed controllable-pitch propeller. Lock Haven to Hayti is not a very long trip, roughly 750 miles, but every fuel stop brought people out to see the new bird, to look, touch, admire, and ask questions. At the destination, it was fun just to land on a dirt runway instead of hard surfaced ones all the time. The only problem with this flight was that it was just too short.

In the summer of 2004, on a family car trip from Colorado to South Carolina, our route passed through Hayti. It wasn't planned that way—it was simply the most convenient route from where we happened to be in that area. As the main street came to the east edge of town, there was the small airport where 52P had been delivered many years before and a large sign advertised Mid-Continent Aircraft Corporation. Out of curiosity, I slowed down, not really expecting to see that particular plane, yet at the same time hoping it would be there. What I saw, I think, was a number of Grumman Ag-Cats (also crop dusters) but no 52P. As we drove on, I liked to imagine it was still there somewhere, maybe back in a hangar someplace or in a shop for a little TLC.

CHAPTER 13

Small World

*M*ost people would agree that the airplane has made the world a much smaller place, made it so much easier to move from one place to another in a very short time. Today people easily travel to places in a car on the interstate in an hour that would have taken pioneers in a covered wagon a week, sometimes more. The world, as large as it is, is also quite small in other ways too. How many times have you run into someone you know in a place or at a time when you never expected them to be within at least of couple of hundred miles of that spot, maybe not within a thousand miles?

Richard Sandys, a friend with whom I taught school at the U.S. Air Force base in Wethersfield, England, told me of a young lady he knew who was planning to be in Europe the same summer we would finish our assignment there. He wrote to her and outlined the itinerary he and another friend and I would probably be following as we toured the Continent after the school year was over, hoping to see her.

Unfortunately, before he could mail the letter, the packers came to pack those things we wanted shipped back to the States as the end of the school year was rapidly approaching and in the process the letter got packed too. (I've even heard of the packers packing people's trash along with the household goods.) He didn't miss the letter until later. Naturally, Richard was disappointed but there really was nothing that could be done about it at that late time. Shortly after school was out, we were in Venice, Italy, gazing with the other tourists at the beauty of the Doges Palace. Suddenly, across the rope barrier dividing the length of a hallway, whom should Richard see but the young lady to whom he had written the letter! Small world!

In late June, back in Lock Haven, one more Pawnee, (N9897P) was picked up for delivery, this time to West Memphis, Arkansas. That trip added about another ten and a half hours to the logbook and not too long after that, I received another call from Bill in Vero Beach about delivering a new Piper Arrow II. Of all places, it was to go to Cheyenne, Wyoming, just forty miles up the road from my home! This was a real winning deal because, once the airplane was delivered, getting home would be a simple matter of having a friend pick me up and I would be home in less than an hour!

Things were looking up. After the Pawnees, the Super Cub, and the Cherokee 140, an Arrow II was a nice offer and it was for a trip about two thirds of the way across the country. It would also be an opportunity to add more time in a retractable-gear plane (one in which the wheels or landing gear fold up inside the fuselage or the wings). So far my retrac time was limited to just enough hours in an Apache a year or two earlier to pick up a multi-engine rating at an airport close to Vero Beach. Once more, Bill gave me a checkout just to be sure I was comfortable with the Arrow and soon it was time to go.

The event leading to the "small world" feeling had begun a couple of hours before as I was waiting for the bus from Melbourne to Vero Beach. I had phoned Bill from the bus station to let him know I was nearly there. Also, I had been watching a certain young man in the bus station, really for no other reason than there were very few people around and one tends to watch other people in a bus station, train station, or airport in such a situation. On the phone, Bill suggested I might keep an eye open for another pilot also on the way. As the man was described, I realized he was the same one I had just been noticing so I introduced myself and we talked airplanes on the bus the rest of the way to Vero. It so happened that he also was delivering a plane to Cheyenne, a Cherokee 235. He left ahead of me and we really had made no specific plans to fly together.

Watching people in a bus station once resulted in another unusual experience in Boston. I happened to be seated on a long bench facing a flight of wide stairs leading to the second floor where the restrooms were located. Shortly, a young man seated himself about three feet away from me and he was casually watching the stairs. Pretty soon I went up to use the restroom but when I went in another man caught my attention, giving the impression that things were not quite as they should be. He was sort of leaning against one wall, facing it, with one arm up in front of his forehead. Sticking out of the back pocket of his jeans was a billfold with money exposed. I decided to come back later and went back and sat down where I had been.

In just a few seconds, there was a slight commotion upstairs. The young man sitting beside me leaped to his feet, whipped out a concealed revolver and rushed up the stairway! Soon he and another man, probably the one I saw in the restroom, were bringing a third man down the stairs in handcuffs! It didn't take much to put two and two together and I supposed that the one I had seen was a police "plant" waiting for someone to try to rob him or maybe make a drug deal and the one seated beside me was his partner. Bus stations in large cities have never been my favorite places to hang out, especially at night! They often seem to attract some very strange characters (no, not delivery pilots)!

Back to the Arrow. It was a wonderful airplane to fly and I was glad for a long trip. The first fuel stop was in Eufala, Alabama. It was raining when I landed and there were cumulus buildups in all quadrants. I made a phone call to a flight service station some miles away to check the weather and who was there but my friend with the 235! I decided to push on and filed to Little Rock, Arkansas, which was a three-hour-twenty-minute trip. The airplane, N1562X, also had autopilot so I spent a little time playing with it. An autopilot was something new to me and it was a nice luxury to have. To do much serious instrument flying, an autopilot would be a tremendous aid. At Little Rock, the plane was fueled and I grabbed a quick sandwich from a machine and filled out a flight plan. Back in the Arrow, I had just started the engine when a line boy came up and signaled me to shut down the engine. "There's a guy over here who wants to see you," he said, and once more, there was the guy flying the 235! After a brief chat about the trip, it was time to move on.

We departed Little Rock at the same time but soon lost contact as the haze was extremely bad and extended upward several thousand feet. Flying west into the sun made it worse. My plan was to reach Dodge City, Kansas, before dark. On delivery trips, insurance policies limited the flying to daytime and to VFR conditions—reasonable for someone else's brand-new airplane. Darkness moved faster than the airplane and as the sun got lower, the visibility became worse—not my idea of fun or a very safe way to fly. I decided to deviate somewhat by turning slightly north so the forward visibility would improve by putting the sun off to the side.. A radio call to flight service advised them of the change in the flight plan and they also agreed to contact the Cherokee 235 pilot to let him know I was headed for Hutchinson so he would not worry if I did not show up shortly after his arrival in Dodge City.

Next morning, I left Hutchinson for what was to be the last leg on to Cheyenne. The weather had other plans, however, for a front lay directly across the intended route and covered a large area of Kansas, Colorado, Nebraska, and Wyoming. For the first part of the flight out of Hutchinson the weather was pretty good so I flew along near the edge of the well-defined front hoping to find a way through.

Going up on top of the cloud cover was out of the question because everyplace I wanted to go toward Cheyenne was either IFR already or going down to minimums. As I cruised along the front, the clouds moved ever lower, forcing me west and south. Finally, I decided to go on to Pueblo, Colorado, located on Interstate 25 which goes straight north to Cheyenne only about an hour and a half away by air.

The last fifty or sixty miles into Pueblo had the Arrow way down to minimum altitude to remain clear of the clouds but I did not consider it a hazardous situation for a couple of reasons. The territory below was now fairly familiar and flat and along the highway below were several smaller airports that could be used if needed.

After landing at Pueblo, I checked the weather again and learned that everything was IFR along the east side of the Rockies because of an upslope condition; it was forecast to remain so the rest of the day and into the next as well. With that information, I chose to find a motel and move on to Cheyenne the next day, if possible.

The one bright spot of the day was Rhonda. She was at the airport and was in the office looking at some photos when I arrived. We began a conversation and soon were chatting like old friends. Rhonda was working toward a flight instructor rating so there was much to talk about easily. Later, she joined me for a bite to eat and it made an otherwise gloomy day much nicer.

In the morning, the clouds were still down but there was a chance of them lifting so I went back to the airport to be ready. Finally, about ten o'clock, some breaks were starting to appear and though Denver at the time was still IFR, Cheyenne was reporting clear so a preflight was done, a flight plan filed, and the trip was ready to continue. I climbed out through a small break in the clouds and soon arrived on top of a beautiful undercast of solid white. North of Denver, the clouds broke and later there was only blue sky above and the familiar ground around Fort Collins below. I radioed Unicom at the Fort Collins Downtown airport and they relayed a message to my friend and partner, Dana, to pick me up in Cheyenne if possible.

Shortly, the plane was landed in Cheyenne in front of Sky Harbor to turn 62X over to the new owner. And who do you suppose had landed about one minute earlier? Yes, the guy delivering the Cherokee 235! Soon Dana arrived and picked me up for the flight home to Fort Collins in our own Cherokee 180. Once more, a great trip and about fifteen more hours of flight time recorded.

To continue the "small world" episode, this airplane, the Arrow II, was used in Cheyenne for about a year then sold to Mr. Bill Strebig, an anesthesiologist in Fort Collins—in fact, a friend and the father of one of my students. He bought it for a lease-back arrangement and it was based at the Fort Collins Downtown Airport, my home base. Bill was not even a pilot at the time, but was an avid outdoorsman.

One day, not knowing anything about my connection with the airplane, and I did not know he had it, he called me to see if I would fly him and two sons, along with a group of other fishermen in several other planes, to Black Lake in Saskatchewan, Canada. What an invitation to a pilot! So, in June of 1976, N1562X and I were together again off to a fishing adventure!

For another fishing trip he asked me to fly him and his two sons from Fort Collins to Hoquiam, Washington, another good trip and an opportunity to see more beautiful country. Not being a great fisherman (I mainly went to Canada just to fly the airplane), I said that while they were fishing for a couple of days, I would take the bus to Portland, Oregon to visit a friend. Bill insisted I take the Arrow II; he was just that kind of a guy. A couple of days later, I picked them up and we had a great trip home.

Later, I used this same Arrow II for the flight training and test to receive my flight instructor rating. Sometimes it really is such a small world!

CHAPTER 14

On the Gauges

As a youngster, I spent several years in the Boy Scout program and believe that one of the reasons that experience continued for about five or six years was because of the new challenges and goals always available. It seemed that with a bit of effort those goals were certainly obtainable and, most of the time, working toward them was as much fun as it was work. One highlight in my young life was the day that I, along with a friend, was awarded the rank of Eagle, scouting's highest rank. We were, to the best of my knowledge, the first in our town to receive it. Whether others have achieved that rank there since, I don't know but hope that a number have done so.

In some ways, flying is similar to the Boy Scout experience. Just as scouting offers various levels of achievement via rank, merit badges and other awards, flying also offers various certificates and ratings one can strive for such as the ATP or ratings like the CFI and CFII. One may pursue other types of goals too; for example, one can learn to fly seaplanes, helicopters, gliders, and balloons. Each scouting rank and merit badge has its own requirements and so do the flight certificates and ratings.

A Boy Scout may choose to achieve only the lowest rank and remain there, or he may move up the ladder, branching out to different fields that interest him. So too, the pilot may choose to move to more advanced certificates and ratings, branching out into areas of particular interest. The highest ranks, whether in scouting or in aviation, are achieved by relatively few people. Perhaps one of the reasons flying can be such a fascinating realm is because of the hundreds of facets and challenges it offers and every flight involves a multitude of skills.

One of the tougher ratings for a pilot to obtain is the instrument rating. With this rating, a pilot is qualified to fly under conditions that restrict others to the ground. Instrument flight refers to a flight made partially or entirely by reference only to the instruments on the panel and when little or no ground can be seen.

During a pilot's earlier training, for both the private and commercial certificates, some instruction is given in flight by instruments only. The purpose of this is not really for intentional flight in IFR conditions but rather to have a safe way of escape should the pilot inadvertently find himself or herself in clouds. This can happen much more easily at night than during the daytime when clouds are easily visible. It can also occur in VFR conditions when there is no visible horizon such as over water on a moonless night.

By the time a pilot has finished training for the instrument rating, it should be possible to take off even when the visibility is zero (though it is not a good idea in case there is a problem and the plane needs to be returned to that airport and landed), climb to altitude, cruise to a destination, descend to within a few hundred feet of the ground, all on instruments, and finally land the airplane. Along with this, one learns proper navigation, radio communications, new altitude requirements, reading new maps and approach charts, and how to handle emergency situations. It is a demanding skill but also a fascinating one. It is also a skill that must be practiced often, like anything, if one is to be good at it.

Three types of tests are involved before the instrument rating can be issued, just as with the pilot certificates. First is a knowledge test (done on a computer), an oral examination, and finally the flight test during which the examiner sees if the student can put it all together and fly various maneuvers without being able to see outside the airplane.

Because there are parts of the U.S. that frequently have a lot of weather with low clouds and poor visibility, the pilot who is rated to fly IFR has a considerable advantage over VFR-only pilots. In many places, weather patterns can change rapidly; in a few minutes an area that was good VFR can alter to become an area where only IFR flight is allowed. The well-prepared pilot is more comfortable in such situations but a poorly prepared one or one whose skills are rusty can easily get into difficulty. Just having the rating doesn't mean he or she will be able to perform all the functions needed to make a safe flight.

Colorado does not normally have many IMC days and when they come, not many are really good for training. It might sound like a plug for the chamber of commerce, but our state does have bright blue skies most of the time. When it is IMC in the summer, it often means there are dangerous thunderstorms nearby and in winter, when fronts come roaring through with high-velocity winds, wind shear, turbulence, and the icing level at or very near ground level, it can be rather nasty.

Since we have far more days with visibility of over fifty miles than we do when the visibility is five or less, most IFR training is done with some kind of view-limiting device such as a visor so the pilot can see only the instrument panel and not see outside. Most IFR-rated pilots will no doubt agree it is actually easier to fly the airplane in actual IMC unless the weather is rather severe. When using a visor you must often turn your head or raise a corner of the visor to see a particular switch or gauge that is easily visible just by moving your eyes when not wearing a visor.

This was the chosen goal, the instrument rating. It was May 1973 and the logbook showed 508 hours when the task began. Once again, I was fortunate to have a very fine instructor, a young, amiable former Vietnam helicopter pilot named Stan Dearhammer. He was patient, taught well, and it was a pleasure to fly with him.

Only a week earlier, my partner and I had sold our Cessna 150, though we had purchased a nice 1967 Cherokee 180 along with a third partner, Dr. Peter Stone, the past December (see Chap. 16). As mentioned earlier, the 150 had been an instrument trainer and had a couple of things the Cherokee could not boast, including a glide slope indicator.

Stan was easy to work with but we worked hard, at least I did under the hood and was usually ready for a break at the end of a lesson. If Stan was ready for one, he didn't show it. Always there was something to do, from the moment we strapped ourselves into the airplane until the engine was shut down after the flight. The maneuvers began simply and became increasingly complex as time went on. First, there was just very basic flight, straight and level, turns, climbs and descents, all of which were later to be done within given limits of speed, altitude, or compass heading. Also there was always some review as well as something new to learn, which not only kept the lessons interesting, it also kept me from thinking I knew all the answers!

We moved on to stalls and recovery from unusual attitudes. Doing such maneuvers without seeing anything but the instruments was different but not really so difficult—it just took practice and a realization of what was happening to the airplane by interpreting what the instruments were indicating. It is in this type of flying that one must learn to not only interpret them but believe what they are saying because relying only on body senses gives false impressions. In a cloud, there is really no way a pilot can know if the craft is right side up or not, straight or turning, climbing or descending.

Once, on a trip in the Cherokee, a friend who does not fly asked about the attitude indicator (gyro horizon). On earlier occasions, he had handled the plane a little bit in straight and level flight so I suggested he close his eyes and try to keep the plane straight and level for only fifteen seconds, relying only on body senses for correct attitude. He really did quite well, for about eight seconds! The end of fifteen seconds found us in a rather nose-high climbing turn to the left. When given the word to open his eyes, they came wide open and he exclaimed "Oh, wow!" He quickly learned what that instrument was for.

Just flying a plane by instruments alone is not as difficult as one might think as long as it is just a matter of going a certain direction at a certain altitude, and speed. The real work is in the fact that there is so much to do besides those basics and while doing other necessary chores the heading, altitude and speed can easily get out of hand. For this reason, an autopilot is a wonderful gadget to have and should be used, especially when in conditions that might be at the limit of what the pilot can handle alone. A pilot who uses autopilot should not rely on it to the extent that, if it goes haywire, he or she cannot fly the plane well without it. A good IFR pilot should be able to fly without autopilot but also know it well enough to use it correctly. The same holds true for GPS.

To give an idea of the complexity that starts creeping into an instrument flight, let's imagine a short trip. Before takeoff, the pilot has carefully determined the route, checked the weather, noted all the radio frequencies to be used, altitude restrictions, gathered airport data, done an extra good preflight inspection and done numerous other things in preparation before even getting in the airplane.

Once aboard, all needed items should be placed where they are readily accessible and in order—the maps, approach plates, pens or pencils, flashlight, emergency checklists, etc. The more preparation a pilot can do on the ground, the less work there is to do in the air. Finally, clearance is received from ATC and written down. Pilots even learn a form of shorthand so information can be written quickly but accurately. The clearance normally gives the destination, route to be followed, altitude to be flown, and other basics. It may be quite simple or, in some cases, somewhat complex. The pilot needs to understand just what those instructions are before departure.

As the plane climbs away from the airport on a given course, it enters the clouds and is now in IMC. Now the pilot must rely solely on the instruments for the safe operation of the aircraft. Of course, there is communication with ATC by radio but ATC cannot actually fly the plane. So our hero sallies forth into the not-so-blue and, if well trained, will have a safe, uneventful journey. Even on an uneventful flight, there are so many details to be taken care of; I respectfully tip my hat to pilots who fly instruments a lot and do it well and safely. It is indeed an accomplishment of which they can be justly proud. Only during the middle part of the flight, at cruise altitude, might the pilot have time to relax a little, but it is still an alert relaxation, monitoring instruments and gauges, holding course, altitude, and speed. It is near the destination that the workload increases significantly and the pilot calls on all learned skills because the airplane is now getting closer to the ground, which cannot be seen, and the danger level increases.

Imagine, if you will, doing all the following in the space of only a few minutes during the approach to landing, and imagine there is only one pilot, no copilot, no crew, as on an airliner to divide these responsibilities:

- Keep the plane on course, turn as necessary
- Maintain the correct altitude, climb or descend as necessary
- Maintain the correct speed, speed up or slow down as needed
- Be aware of where the plane is at all times in relation to the airport
- Read and interpret the approach charts
- Change radio frequencies as needed and use the microphone
- Adjust the engine fuel mixture
- Adjust throttle and propeller settings
- Scan the instruments to see that all is in order
- Switch fuel tanks as needed
- Watch time for turns, or estimating time to a certain point
- Double-check minimum altitudes
- Write new instructions that may come over the radio
- Watch for indications of ice formation
- Adjust cowl and wing flaps
- Lower the landing gear
- Know what to do immediately if the airport is not visible at minimum altitude
- Do all of the above in a cool, calm, professional manner

And, added to this list, we might throw in some turbulence, maybe an ill passenger or a rapidly dwindling fuel supply, a critical instrument that chooses this moment to quit working, or any other number of things that might make the flight less than normal. You can begin to appreciate the kind of person who can handle it, can take charge, and do what needs to be done.

The next time you are a passenger, whether in a smaller aircraft or a large airliner that makes a safe flight when the weather is lousy, take a moment to say a word of thanks to the pilot—let him or her know you have some idea of what it takes to do the job well.

Let's not forget the people on the ground that do a great deal to help pilots on IFR flight plans reach their destinations safely. Most of the time, the planes the ATC specialists are working are visible to them only on their radar screens and, most of the time, they are in direct radio contact with them. Though the pilot-in-command has the final authority as to how the airplane is flown, ATC may offer suggestions or sometimes give directives to help pilots avoid dangerous situations such as bad weather, other aircraft, or collision with terrain, all of which could also lead to serious health hazards. They may give new altitudes, new headings, request changes in speed, request a holding pattern or changes of radio frequencies, and changes in which runway to use.

For the pilot flying on instruments without the aid of an autopilot, a call from ATC can sometimes be a rather hectic time. Often, but not always, there is information that should be written down simply because there is too much to remember at one time or it may be information that will not be used for a while and could be forgotten. Trying to fly the airplane and write the information at the same time without an autopilot is a bit like trying to pat your head and rub your stomach at the same time and for some people that's nearly a physical impossibility! Sometimes the information to be written is very brief and at other times it may seem like you're hearing something as long as the Gettysburg Address.

There are shorthand symbols that can be used but even those need to be practiced so they will be right at your fingertips when needed. There is probably a government regulation somewhere requiring ATC people, along with the tower personnel mentioned earlier, to complete a course in auctioneer school to learn to speak at the proper speed to communicate with pilots! With practice, one can learn to write the information in a fairly understandable form the first time it is heard.

Though it might be a little embarrassing to ask ATC to repeat a direction a couple of times, it is far better to do that than to assume you understood and blunder into another airplane or thunderstorm cell or a mountain. By the same token I believe ATC would probably save more of their time and tie up the radio for less time, particularly when speaking to pilots in small airplanes, if they would simply speak more slowly so pilots would understand the first time, not have to ask for repeats or cause an embarrassed pilot to fly merrily on his way on an assumption that what was heard was correct.

It has been said that the bigger a plane is, the easier it is to fly. In many ways this may be true since larger aircraft usually have an autopilot system or copilot and flight engineer to monitor the progress of the flight along with the pilot. Normally, there would also be two sets of most instruments.

The smaller the plane, the more work the pilot must do alone. This means the pilot of a small plane must be good at what he is doing in IMC. One should recognize his or her limits and those of the aircraft so that if a situation arises that appears beyond those limits, actions can be taken quickly to reduce the situation to one that can be handled safely. That might include landing at an airport other than the intended destination that might be somewhat inconvenient but certainly much safer. The chances of ending up at the destination alive are increased by a large margin.

In 1976, while returning from the Canadian fishing trip in the Arrow II mentioned in the previous chapter, I had an opportunity to see how quickly situations can change and go from normal to abnormal. We were loaded with people, baggage, fuel, fish, and lots of good memories of several days in the wilderness. The clouds were very low the morning we left Black Lake but I was soon able to contact a Norcanair (Northern Canadian Air) pilot who said he was in and out of the clouds at only 4,000 feet. Since it was early in the morning, I did not expect the clouds to extend very high and, with the Norcanair report, figured to be in the clear above the clouds at about 5,000 feet and proceeded to climb. We were over a wilderness area, off any normal air routes and out of contact with anyone on the ground at the time.

At 5,000 feet we were still on solid instruments so the climb continued. It began to look brighter above but that was misleading. At 11,000 we were not only still in cloud but now were beginning to pick up some ice, not a fun place to be. In addition, I had neglected an important item, turning on the pitot heat which I should have done immediately upon entering the clouds or just before. Probably the main reason it was overlooked was simply a lack of enough IFR experience. With no heat, the airspeed indicator gradually dropped to zero and my initial reaction was to believe we were approaching a stall so the nose was lowered to gain speed. Other instruments indicated normal flight except the airspeed indicator. Then it occurred to me what the problem was—ice in the pitot tube. Fooling around in this condition was getting close to the limits of my capabilities and those of the airplane and if things did not change quickly, we stood a good chance of making a nasty mess on the beautiful Canadian countryside.

Quickly the landing gear and flaps were lowered for a faster descent and by carefully watching the instruments, I could tell if the plane was in a reasonable attitude and the speed in a reasonable range. A quick check of the map gave an idea of the elevation of the terrain below, at least as nearly as the position could be estimated and fortunately, the terrain in that part of Saskatchewan is quite flat. Before long the airspeed indicator was working properly and soon the pleasant sound of rain started hitting the windshield, which meant we were back again in warmer air. Shortly thereafter patches of ground appeared below so we circled down in an opening and leveled off below the clouds. Returning to the proper heading, we certainly enjoyed the countryside with more than a short time earlier, at least I did.

Though I had made some mistakes that got us into this situation, I was very thankful for some excellent training that paid off when needed and allowed me to maintain control of the airplane instead of losing it. I was also thankful to the Lord and my guardian angel who were probably thinking something like "Oh, no, he's done it again, we'd better give him some help." At times like that, one accepts all the help available.

The airplane owner, Bill Strebig, beside me in the right seat, was also quite helpful by monitoring some instruments and even though he was not a pilot at the time, at one point calmly indicated that the heading was not where it should be. This was very important because it could have been the beginning of a deadly spiral dive, but as long as the course was held steady it meant we were not turning, thus another indication that the wings were level. The remainder of the trip was without incident but the experience made me a wiser and better pilot.

111

Well, back to the training that gave a happy ending to the story just told. The training with Stan finally came to an end after many good hours and a few frustrating ones. The Cherokee 180 we had was only minimally equipped for instrument flight. It had only one VOR receiver, one Comm (communication) radio, and an older ADF, but nothing like a second radio, marker beacon, or DME, nor did it have area nav equipment, and you can forget GPS, it wasn't even available yet.

Working with only one radio meant lots of knob twisting as needed to switch back and forth between frequencies. Everything seemed to need more attention. Maybe that made me a better pilot, having to do it the hard way. For pilots today who train with all the goodies, I really hope they can function with just the basics if, while in instrument conditions, some vital piece of equipment suddenly decides to pack up and head south. Good training is worth its weight in gold.

Occasionally, my friend and partner, Dana, would fly with me to be the safety pilot so I could put on the visor and practice and sometimes I did the same for him. He would give me flight problems to solve such as putting the plane into an unusual attitude and telling me to recover to level flight or giving headings and altitudes to maintain. Near the airport, he would be the controller, giving vectors that would eventually have the airplane lined up on final approach and nearly to the ground before letting me lift the visor and land. That all added up to build confidence.

Sometimes Dana got a little mischievous and did things to keep me on the ball. He might switch a radio to a wrong frequency to see if it would be noticed—not unlike a real situation in which a pilot might accidentally put in a wrong frequency. At another time, when I was not watching, the flaps might be lowered a few degrees to see if I could figure out why the airspeed was not what it should be. Yet another trick was to pull a fuse part way out to simulate a burned out one and see how long it took to notice the problem and figure out a solution, which might involve replacing a fuse. Good training! Thanks, Dana.

In preparation for the written exam (knowledge exam), there were hours of ground school. Suffice it to say that the exam results came in the mail about a week later and the score was good enough to go take the flight test. The test was taken in Cheyenne and consisted of an oral exam and the flight itself which was almost too easy after all the training. It included a short cross-country during which many of the items practiced were tested and it ended with two different types of approaches, all done under the visor.

A heavy, bright blue line outlines the "remarks" column of the logbook where it is noted that the instrument test was passed satisfactorily. I had told Stan that if I passed the test on the first attempt, he and his wife would be treated to a steak dinner. Well, that steak was delicious! Thank you, Stan, for sticking with me to achieve a long-sought-after goal.

CHAPTER 15

T—for "Two"

Christmas attracts many people to Colorado for some of the best skiing in the world. Fort Collins, where I was living at the time, sits just out of the Rockies on the east side, sixty miles north of Denver and only two or three hours by car from some of the best slopes. Part of my winter vacation in 1973 was spent visiting family and friends, part on the ski slopes, and part wondering what to do with the several days remaining.

Many "flatlanders" also come to Colorado to ski, some by private plane and many of those are twin-engine craft. Colorado not only boasts some of the finest skiing but also some of the highest mountains in the country (fifty-four peaks over 14,000 feet) and the highest airport in the U.S. at Leadville located at an elevation of over 9,000 feet above sea level.

Much of the eastern plains area of Colorado has an elevation of approximately 4,000 feet and Denver, because of its elevation, is often referred to as the Mile High City. For many pilots, the only way to fly at these elevations is to have a plane with more than one engine. Since most of Colorado's airports are higher than many pilots cruise going from one airport to another in lower states, twins and turbo-charged singles and twins are common sights in this part of the U.S.

Maybe that was partly why an ad in *Trade-A-Plane* caught my eye during one of those vacation days. It offered a multi-engine rating for only $199 to be done in only two days. (You can see how prices have changed in the intervening years!) Now, I enjoy a bargain as much as the next guy and so decided to do some checking. There were now only four days remaining in the vacation so it did seem like sort of a crazy scheme, but then quite a few things done on the spur of the moment in my life have turned out to be some of the most enjoyable.

I phoned the company in Florida that placed the ad and they assured me that the job could be done in two days but that it would take a lot of work. After giving some background information and asking for a spot to be reserved in the schedule, I got busy at home. With some experience already at leaving on short notice, arrangements were made for a commercial flight, a few clothes put together, traveler's checks obtained, and, within about three hours, I was gone.

Not many hours later, I stepped off a plane at Miami International. Getting a motel room was a bit of a problem as the Orange Bowl was being played then. Success finally came and evening found me on the motel balcony, under a beautiful Florida sky and an eighty-degree temperature, reflecting on what had taken place in just the past half a day and contemplating what would be happening in the next two days.

In the morning, a taxi took me to the Opa-Locka airport and I began searching for the Pro Air office. Finally, at the end of a long row of assorted older buildings and offices, a small sign directed me to it. The office was small and rather bare. A counter divided the room but nobody was there—no chic secretary or flight schedule people, no instructors in uniform, nobody.

After a few minutes wait, I went out to look around a bit. It was still fairly early and not much seemed to be going on anywhere. Later, I returned to the office and found a gentleman behind the counter so I explained who I was and the purpose of the visit. Somehow, in this huge, multi-level organization, my name had not been put on any schedule, but it was finally decided that they could "work me in." The instructor was to be a young guy by the name of Dave Snyder. We spent a short time talking about the upcoming lessons and covered some basics that could be done on the ground.

He then led me to the flight line and it became more apparent why the rating was being offered at such a bargain price! Our plane was an older (even in 1973) PA-23 Piper Apache. N3454P looked like it had been "rode hard and put away wet" as the cowboys would say. Older airplanes are really okay in many respects as long as they have been well maintained. Many are flying today that are thirty, forty, and fifty years old and probably still have some pretty good life left in them. The Apache was one of the most popular twins for multi-engine training because it was not too expensive to purchase and is a pretty forgiving airplane to fly.

A walk-around inspection revealed nothing out of the ordinary; it is a simple operation. It was on the inside that a few things seemed a little odd, like several holes in the instrument panel where there were no instruments.

"What goes here?" I asked a couple of times and Dave's reply was very reassuring.

"Don't worry about it, we don't need that."

Thanks a lot! At least there were a few essentials like an airspeed indicator and an altimeter.

117

We had already discussed some of the more important features of the airplane, the maneuvers to be learned, several basic speeds to be known, and some emergency procedures. Once inside the plane, they were reviewed with emphasis on minimum-control airspeed, best single-engine climb speed, and engine-out performance and procedure. Then we fired up the engines and taxied out for takeoff. As at Vero Beach, it was wonderful to see the Atlantic just after takeoff, not a sight we get to see in Colorado.

Since time was valuable, we didn't waste any and climbed right away to altitude to begin some air work. It looked strange on the altimeter to see that our working altitude of 3,000 feet was about two thousand lower than the airport elevation at home. Dave had trained quite a few pilots in the Apache and seemed to know his stuff. We worked on slow flight, flight characteristics at near minimum controllable speed, approach and departure stalls, and engine-out procedures. A lot was accomplished in a relatively short time, yet it did not seem rushed, just constantly busy.

That first day we also did seven touch-and-go landings, some normal and some with power on one engine reduced to idle. We did go-arounds (when the airplane does not come down to touch the runway but at some point climbs and goes around the traffic pattern for another landing attempt) in normal configuration and some with simulated problems where the wheels had to be lowered or raised manually with a hand pump located between the front seats.

The trick to all of this was to be careful to maintain adequate speed and control of the airplane while attending to other operations. The following day was more of the same, air work and five more takeoffs and landings.

An inspector was available on the field so that same afternoon of the second day he and I sat down and he gave me the

118

oral exam, then we moved on to the flight test. The inspector, J. H. Dunaway, Jr., ran through all the maneuvers that had been practiced with Dave. The flight test presented no real problems; even though the training had not involved many hours, it was still fresh and that probably had a lot to do with making the test easier. Very often, a pilot receives training for some level of proficiency, then for any number of reasons must postpone the flight test for several days, a week or two, maybe a month or longer and unless some refresher training is done the flight test could then be considerably more difficult.

Forty-five minutes after takeoff, we landed back at Opa-Locka and I became, for a while anyway, the country's newest multi-engine-rated pilot. By six o'clock that same evening I was again at Miami International and on the way back to Denver. I tried not to think of the expense that might have been incurred if, after coming all that distance, for some reason such as bad weather, mechanical difficulties, lack of an inspector when needed, or scheduling problems, the feat had not been accomplished. It was a very nice feeling to know that the decision had been made, the action had been taken and the result was a multi-engine rating in my pocket. It was a very pleasant trip home.

Unfortunately, there was a down side to all this as I was soon to learn. Shortly after returning to Colorado, I went to my home airport to rent a twin (two-engine plane) to start building some time and ran into a brick wall (not with an airplane), figuratively speaking. Because of the insurance, they would not rent out the twin until I had at least two hundred hours of twin time and I couldn't get the time without renting the airplane. It was the old vicious circle all over again.

There were a few alternatives, to be sure. One, I could just go out and buy my own twin and fly it but the decimal point on the price tags always seemed to be several places out of position to the right. Secondly, signing up with Uncle Sam for a few years might have been a possibility but it, too, had some disadvantages. As a result, the rating has gotten a lot of wear just from being carried around in my billfold but not from being used.

Fortunately, one of my good friends in Fort Collins, Bill Vigor, has owned several nice twin-engine planes including a Beechcraft Baron, a Cessna 340 (N7771Q), and the exceptionally nice Beechcraft Duke. On several occasions, he has invited me to accompany him on trips and given me a chance to gain some experience with his airplanes, and for that I am still very grateful. Thanks, Bill!

In addition to being a pilot, Bill is also a great outdoorsman who has hunted and fished in many different parts of the world. He is the one who organized the fishing trips we took to Saskatchewan.

At least the goal had been set and reached, another aviation challenge had been met.

CHAPTER 16

N9759J

My partner on the Cessna 150, Dana, and I had been toying with the idea of moving up to a little nicer airplane. What pilot has not done that before? If you have a two-place plane you want a four-place, if you have 180 hp you want more, if you have one engine you want two. We felt that, with a third partner, we would be able to find one within a reasonable price range and not be too limited on use of the plane with only three people flying it so we started doing some window shopping. The decision was that, if we found what we wanted and could afford it, the purchase could be made even though we still owned the 150; it could be sold and much of our cash could be regained.

To make a long story short, we did find a very nice 1967 Piper Cherokee 180 in the local area with low time on the airframe and on the engine. We were also very fortunate to find Dr. Peter Stone as our third partner. He had recently moved to the Fort Collins area, already possessed a private certificate, and was an extremely easy person to get along with. Many

partnerships do not work out well because of personality con-
flicts or disagreement about scheduling and flying the airplane.
The three of us never had such difficulties.

As might be expected, the Cherokee went into the hangar
that had housed 23G and 23G was assigned a tie-down spot
outside, almost like an old toy that is tossed aside when a child
gets a new one. Fortunately, the 150 did sell four months later
and things worked out well. At the time, my logbook showed
about 440 hours. This airplane was to be our magic carpet,
our time machine. We bought it for $10,000 and sold it for the
same price with a high-time engine eight years later. Today,
a nice 1967 Cherokee 180 sells for approximately $40,000 or
$50,000. It performed wonderfully well, needing hardly any-
thing more than regular inspections and minor maintenance.
I believe the most expensive thing we had done on it was to
put in new fuel cell bladders.

In addition to a lot of local flights for pleasure as well as
for later training, the Cherokee was taken on many marvelous
trips, some very short, some very long. A few shorter flights
included taking my parents to Cheyenne for lunch to show
off the new machine, a trip to Colorado Springs with my good
friend Clyde and his son David and a trip to North Platte,
Nebraska, with my good friend Tim (the one along on the
President Johnson escapade). At the restaurant at the North
Platte airport, I happened to meet a gentleman from Haxtun
whom I had known for some years. He also had flown in for
a bite to eat. Pilots refer to such flights as "hundred-dollar
hamburger" flights.

Paging through the log recalls many wonderful memories.
One was a day when Clyde's adult Sunday school class members were treated to rides, a total of three flights, and the first
time up for some. Another with the principal of my school and
his wife and several with friends from church. For my mother,

a trip to Grand Island, Nebraska, normally an eight-hour car trip, was made in three in the Cherokee.

One evening, I took two teachers from my school to Denver's Stapleton Airport where we enjoyed a very nice dinner in the terminal, watching all the airport activity. As we approached to land on the very long runway, I chose to simply fly the plane about halfway down the runway before touching down in order to save taxiing time. While I was still holding the plane in the air, just a couple of feet off the ground, one of them said. "Wow, Jim, that was really a smooth landing!" Would that all my landings were so smooth!

Dana and I took a medium-sized trip north to South Dakota to fly over the Badlands and to have a bird's eye view of Mount Rushmore and not long after that, a trip south to visit Carlsbad Caverns in New Mexico. This is one of the wonders of the private airplane. Trips such as these we would normally hardly consider by car just because of the amount of time they take. On the ground, by the time one counts all the speed limits, stop lights, and turns one must make, the average speed is greatly reduced from normal highway speed. The airplane need not heed highway speed limits, stop lights, rush hour, or even curves and sharp turns; it normally proceeds at cruise speed and in a straight line.

As mentioned in an earlier chapter, this was the plane I used to train in and test in for the instrument rating which was completed in June of 1973. A few entries show up as being flown on an IFR flight plan but there was very little actual instrument flight involved.

A school science class and its teacher is another entry as well as another trip back to Texas, to Houston this time with the same Haxtun friend, Leon Atkins, whom I had taken to Texas before in the 150. One this trip, we found a great steakhouse in Dallas that had an all-you-can-eat steak night while we were there and we sure did take advantage of that! This was an especially memorable evening because two people who joined us for dinner were two local teachers with whom I had taught in Newfoundland about ten years earlier! Without the airplane, such a reunion probably never would have happened.

A weekend jaunt in October of '73, again with Tim and two other friends to Santa Fe, New Mexico, just to do some sightseeing, is a good example of how the airplane can widen one's horizons and shrink the world.

Quite a few passengers in the Cherokee were people who had never flown before, and they all loved it. It is very satisfying to do something nice like that for people and give them an experience they enjoy and remember. Almost exactly thirty years ago, as this is being written, I gave a first ride to a friend with whom I used to teach and who has been a successful real estate salesman for many years. We still keep in touch from time to time and just recently he was still marveling at that flight.

About this same time, I was doing a little bit of flying for an organization called Wings of Faith, which flew pastors and other church personnel to various sites for conferences or other church related business. The organization even purchased an older Cessna 170 that was to be delivered from Fort Collins to San Diego after having a little face-lifting done to make it more attractive. As one of the few locals with taildragger experience, it was my privilege, along with a pastor friend, to make that trip and turn it over to the new owners.

On another occasion, Steve and Martha McNeal, both teachers and members at my church, and Martha's sister, needed to go to Kansas City for a conference . They did not wish to drive so the faithful Cherokee was put into service again and it saved them many hours. A nice sidelight to that trip was that, after dropping them off, I had some free time and a flight of less than an hour took me to Wolff Harbor, Missouri, on the Lake of the Ozarks where a leisurely lunch was enjoyed at a restaurant right on the water.

Another destination with a fellow teacher, Bob Warner, and his wife who went along for the weekend in Santa Fe, was the famous Harold Warp Pioneer Village in Minden, Nebraska—one of the finest museums of early American small town life in the country. Bob was a woodshop teacher at the first school I worked at as well as one of the local golf pros. The Warners thoroughly enjoyed these excursions to see something new and different and do it the easy way. The airport in Minden is within easy walking distance of Pioneer Village. It is an outstanding place for a family adventure. Put it on your fly-in list if you have never been there.

By now 1974 had arrived and trips in the Cherokee began to get interrupted as I began making the delivery trips for Ferry Service Company. It was a wonderful, wonderful time. When not flying our own Cherokee, there was a delivery to be made, a total of nineteen delivery trips, including one in a new Piper Tomahawk painted like a Fresca soda can as an advertising gimmick. It was delivered from Pennsylvania to California. That one sure got people's attention at the airports where I dropped in for fuel!

Along the way, I did receive an offer to deliver one new Cessna. It was a six-place 206 from the Kansas factory to Miami, Florida. That trip took place in the winter. It was a great trip. I very much enjoyed flying the 206, in fact, I once flew one to Black Lake, Saskatchewan on another fishing trip. The 206 is a good airplane and a real load-hauler. I would have enjoyed delivering more of them.

Again with friend Tim and the Warners aboard, we headed north to Montana to visit Glacier National Park, an area of outstanding natural beauty. On the return we took in an old-time melodrama in Jackson Hole, Wyoming, also famous for scenic mountain vistas. One does not need an entire two-week vacation to drive several hundred miles to such places, spend a couple of days, and then spend lots of time driving home. It's surprising how much one can do in just a three-day weekend by air.

Every year in late September, my hometown of Haxtun puts on a Corn Festival to celebrate the harvest of wheat, corn, and other crops. Usually it includes a parade, (sometimes a very long and interesting one), street games for kids and adults, store window displays, and other activities that might include a football game, a dance, an auto demolition derby, tractor pulls, and a crowning of royalty. Street stands sell great things to eat, including delicious homemade pies, hamburgers, ice cream, and other goodies to make it a festive occasion.

One year, my parents went along in the Cherokee from Fort Collins, just over a one-hour flight, so they could visit friends they had known there for many years. That day, my logbook shows several flights to give rides to some of the local people whom I also had known since my childhood. For some, it was their first time up.

Only three weeks later, with my parents, we returned to Chappell, Nebraska, not far north of Haxtun, to attend the funeral of one of my dad's sisters. By using the airplane, we were able to go in comfort and spend more time with relatives than would have been the case had we driven.

For Christmas vacation in 1974, Dana, Tim, and I loaded up the "time machine" and headed south, way south to Miami for a bit of fun in the sun. At one point, between Oklahoma City and Vicksburg, Mississippi, we picked up a nice tailwind that sped us along with a ground speed of 178 mph (not knots), not bad for a plane that normally cruises at about 120.

Lest you get the idea that I had unlimited funds to do all this flying, let me assure you, that was not the case, particularly on a public teacher's salary. Usually expenses were divided with the passengers and I paid an equal share.

By midsummer of 1975 the logbook showed about 950 hours of flight time, 950 of the most enjoyable hours of my life spread over quite a few years.

Before reaching the magical thousand-hour milestone, several other memorable flights are recorded. Looking at the log, I see a long flight with my friends Dana and Tim from Fort Collins to Washington state, where my sister Betty lives, and from there over the border to Victoria, British Colombia. That trip included flying past Mount St. Helen's (before it erupted) and past Mount Rainier, both offering spectacular views, as well as flying along the beautiful Oregon and Washington coastlines. On such trips, Dana and I divided piloting duties and flight time logged.

Finally, on November 15, 1975, the log shows an entry of only a twenty-minute flight but it was done for a singular purpose. Before takeoff, the logbook showed a total of 999 hours, forty minutes. After landing, I happily logged flight hour number one thousand.

In the years that followed, there were many more terrific flights. They were interrupted again in the 1980s and 1990s when I returned overseas to teach in the Marshall Islands on the tiny island of Kwajalein in the South Pacific for two years and after that to Seoul, South Korea, for another five.

My flying has almost come to a halt since returning from Korea but I still have hopes of doing more. Today, the total flight time recorded in the logbooks is just under 1,800 hours, only a beginning compared to many pilots whose time is in the tens of thousands of hours.

It has been a wonderful privilege to see so much of the United States via small airplane. Our country has such a huge variety of scenery. I have traveled to some extent in all of the fifty states by one means of transportation or another but doing so by air is a special and thrilling experience. If I were never able to fly again, I could not complain because of having already enjoyed it so much.

So this is my story of flight. I hope it will encourage you who have never stretched your wings very far from home to enjoy the wonderful world of flight even more. Hopefully, it will encourage you who are considering learning to fly and you who are just now beginning to experience the thrill of flight to do so with great care and safety so that all your stories of flying will have happy endings.

Appendix

ircraft mentioned in the book listed by manufacturer, type and N number, if known. If anyone reading this book knows the current whereabouts of any of the airplanes listed, the author would enjoy hearing from you.

Aeronca: 7AC (N2107E), Champion 7FC Tri-Traveler (N7563B), (N7509B), (N7582B)

Beechcraft: Beech 18, Bonanza

Boeing 727, 747

Cessna: 120 (N1770N), (N3754V), 140 (N2397V,), (N2987N), 150 (N8523G), (N7939E), (N5912R), (N7869E), (N7863E), (N5718F), (N6155T), (N8409J), (N22955J), (N60249), (N55162), (N51095), (N22001), 170 (N2629D), 172

(N3934F), (N4007F), (N7034T), (N3056V), (N6303L), (N2569L), (N7770G), 175 (N7060E)

Convair

Douglas: DC-3

Fornaire (Forney Industries): Ercoupe (N3016G)

McDonald-Douglas: MD-80

(military): F-15, F-100 Super Sabre

Piper: Apache (N3454P), Arrow II (N1562X), Brave (N9952P), Caribbean (N33082), Cherokee 140 (N5010W), (N1442X), (N9875W), (N6409W), (N7375J), Cherokee 180 (N9759J),Colt (N—96Z) (?), J-3 Cub (N42657), Pawnee (XB-TEX), (XB-KOY), (N9897P), Super Cruiser, Super Cub (N6724L), Tomahawk, Tri-Pacer (N602A), (N8849D), (N10335), (N8549D), (N3308Z)

Taylorcraft: BC-12D (N36324), L-2 (NC52178)

Index

Vero Beach, FL 11, 88, 89, 94, 95, 118

W

Warner, Bob 125

White, Aaron (Ron) 9, 10, 21

Y

Young, Dan 3

Glossary

AD: airworthiness Directive: information relating to a specific item on a specific make and model of airplane which must be repaired or replaced for the plane to be considered airworthy

ATP: airline transport pilot: pilot certificate rated above a commercial certificate. It is required for captains flying commercial airliners.

Aileron: small movable control surface near the outer end of the wing that allows the pilot to bank the airplane; left and right ailerons work opposite of each other—when one goes up, the other goes down

Aircraft number: (N number) similar to the VIN number or license plate on a car; all airplanes registered in the U.S. have registrations beginning with N, followed by the numbers and often another letter—for example, Cherokee N9759J is referred to over the radio as Cherokee November niner seven five niner Juliette. (usually, after the initial radio call, further transmissions use only the last three number/letter combination for brevity, such as Cherokee 59J [five niner Juliette] or possibly just 59J [five niner Juliette]

CAA: Civil Aeronautics Administration: forerunner of the present FAA, the official government agency governing all U.S. civilian aviation

Certificate: often referred to as a license; issued to pilots who pass official FAA exams; grants piloting privileges within the limits set by the government; includes private, commercial, and ATP levels.

Checkout: a flight with an instructor to see that a pilot is proficient in a different make or model of airplane; does not require any test—for example, a pilot qualified to fly a single-engine land plane, such as he Cessna 172 only needs a checkout to be able to fly a Cessna 182 or a Beechcraft Bonanza since both are single-engine land planes.

Checkpoint: something on the earth's surface such as a town, river, bridge, lake, or racetrack that a pilot may identify to establish or confirm the plane's location during flight

CFI: certified flight instructor

CFII: certified instrument flight instructor; one qualified to teach people to fly an airplane by reference to instruments alone; sometimes referred to as a "double I"

Colt's Neck VOR: name of a radio navigation facility located near New York City

Cumulus clouds: clouds having vertical build-up (see Stratus clouds)

DME: distance measuring equipment: a piece of navigation equipment that tells the pilot the distance and, if the plane is so equipped, the time to a navigation facility tuned in on the aircraft radio

Downwind leg: part of the rectangular traffic pattern airplanes fly around the airport prior to landing; opposite to the direction of landing; it is followed by the base leg which is ninety degrees to the runway and finally the final approach leg which is lined up with the runway before touchdown.

FAA: Federal Aviation Administration: official government agency in charge of all civilian aircraft activity in the U.S.

Flaps: small movable control surfaces at the back (trailing edge) of the wing near the fuselage; used to give additional lift to the wing for takeoff and to slow the airplane for landing; they allow a steeper descent with little or no increase in speed

Gauges: slang term used to refer to the flight instruments such as the altimeter and airspeed indicator different from normal usage as with "fuel gauges"

Ground school: instruction given on the ground to people before or after they begin flight lessons; includes topics such as weather, weight and balance, physiology, and navigation

IFR: instrument flight rules: rules governing flight by reference only to instruments when the ground is not visible; can also refer to flight on an IFR flight plan, following IFR rules even though the airplane is not in clouds

IMC: instrument meteorological conditions: refers to weather conditions in which visibility and/or cloud ceilings are so low that flight must be made by instruments part or all of the time

Logbook: official record book in which a pilot records pertinent information of each flight—date, aircraft make and model, point of departure and point of landing, duration, day or night, solo or dual, VFR or IFR and other information as needed

Microburst: strong vertical downward wind that spreads out as it reaches the earth's surface; usually associated with thunderstorm activity

Multi-engine: refers to any aircraft having more than one engine; one with two engines is commonly called a twin

Pilotage: a method of navigation by which the pilots keeps track of the position by watching the ground, following rivers, roads, identifying towns, etc.; may or may not include use of a map

Section lines: straight roads running north-south one mile apart intersected by roads running east-west also one mile apart enclosing a section or one square mile of land

Short field takeoff/landing: a takeoff or landing during which the airplane rolls along the ground for a shorter distance than normal; may be due to obstacles such as trees or buildings at one or both ends of the runway

Soft field takeoff/landing: a takeoff or landing on a surface that may be soft because of rain, mud, tall grass, snow, etc.

Stratus clouds: clouds that are basically horizontal with little or no vertical development

Taildragger: an airplane having a small wheel on the tail assembly in addition to the larger main wheels further forward; also called a tailwheel airplane

Touch-and-go: refers to an airplane that touches down on the runway for a landing but instead of stopping, power is added and the airplane takes off again; normally used for takeoff and landing practice

Trade-A-Plane: popular aviation trade newspaper published in Crossville, TN, advertises aircraft for sale or to purchase, aviation-related parts and accessories, flight schools, maintenance, etc.

Traffic pattern: rectangular flight path airplanes normally follow around the airport after takeoff or in preparation for landing (see downwind leg)

Tricycle gear: refers to the wheel arrangement on an airplane having a smaller wheel under the nose and the larger main wheels further aft (see taildragger)

Undercast: clouds below the flight altittude of an airplane

VFR: visual flight rules: rules governing flight when the pilot can see the ground; forward visibility and cloud ceilings are higher than the limits restricting flight to IFR

VOR: visual omnirange: a type of navigation using a ground facility that sends out a radio signal on a certain frequency and an instrument in the airplane allowing the pilot to fly to or from that facility by following a needle or similar indicator

Vertical stabilizer: the vertical, fixed part of the airplane tail assembly; the movable rudder is attached to it

Wheel fairings: sometimes called wheel covers or wheel pants; usually metal, fiberglass or plastic coverings over the wheels to streamline them and for aesthetic purposes

About the Author

Today, Jim Kasparek lives in Colorado Springs, Colorado with his wife and daughter. He retired in the spring of 2004 from a forty-year career as a secondary teacher, primarily of French. His other aviation-related book, *THE RULEBREAKER,* just published, is a fiction novel about a new pilot who causes a midair collision over the Colorado Rocky Mountains near Colorado Springs because he disregards the rules of safe flight. Jim is involved in his church and travel continues to be a favorite activity.

He may be contacted at Bright Future Publications, P.O. Box 75339, Colorado Springs, CO 80970 or by e-mail at kasparek@frii.com.

ORDER FORM

THE FIRST THOUSAND HOURS

To order additional copies of this book, simply fill in the information below and mail it with your check or money order to:

BRIGHT FUTURE PUBLICATIONS
P.O. Box 75339
Colorado Springs, CO 80970
kasparek@frii.com

(or call toll-free WinePress Publishing 1-(877) 421-7323)

YES, I would like to order _____ (quantity) copies of *THE FIRST THOUSAND HOURS* at $14.99 each. Please add $ 3.50 each for shipping and handling.

(Colo. residents add $ .43 sales tax per book)
Total enclosed: $ _____

Name: _____

Address: _____

City / Town: _____

State: _____ Zip: _____

Phone: (   ) _____
Please allow three weeks for delivery

ORDER FORM

THE RULEBREAKER

To order additional copies of this book, simply fill in the information below and mail it with your check or money order to

BRIGHT FUTURE PUBLICATIONS
P.O. Box 75339
Colorado Springs, CO 80970
kasparek@frii.com

(or call toll-free WinePress Publishing 1-(877) 421-7323)

YES, I would like to order _____ (quantity) copies of *THE RULEBREAKER* at $16.99 each. Please add $ 4.00 each for shipping and handling.

(Colo. residents add $ .43 sales tax per book)
Total enclosed: $ _____

Name: _____

Address: _____

City / Town: _____

State: _____ Zip: _____

Phone: (_____) _____
Please allow three weeks for delivery

To order additional copies of

The **First**
Thousand Hours
A Pilot's Log

Have your credit card ready and call:

1-877-421-READ (7323)

or please visit our web site at
www.pleasantword.com

Also available at:
www.amazon.com
and
www.barnesandnoble.com

Printed in the United States
56309LVS00003BA/180